Feng Shui

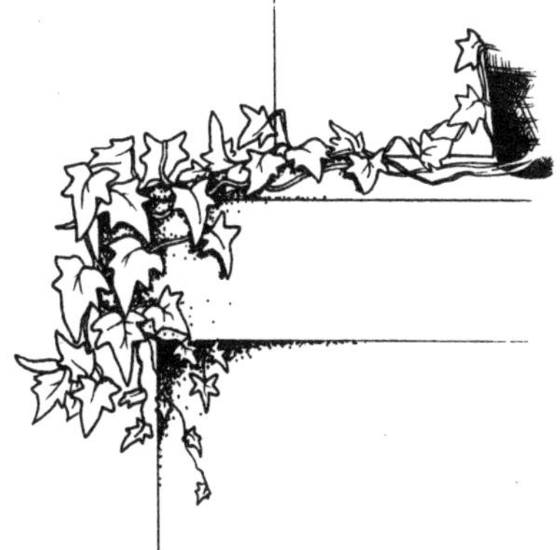

Going with the Flow

Lina Visconti

Feng Shui, Going with The Flow
by Lina Visconti

published by:

TM Publications
9251-8 Yonge Street, Unit 121
Richmond Hill, Ontario L4C 9T3

Library of Congress
Cataloging-in-Publication Data
on file with the publisher
Feng Shui, Going With The Flow
I S B N 009684391-1-X

First edition 1999
98 99 00 10 11 12 13 14

Dedicated to
my
Mom and Dad
Fiorina and Mario Turco

ACKNOWLEDGMENTS

I would like to thank Tom Mallioras for his ongoing technical and moral support and persitance in the creation of book number two. A special thank you to my assistant, Jennifer Volpe for all her dedication and commitment to this project.

Thank you to my husband Rick and my children Maryanne and John Mark for their love and support.

Many thanks to the talented Stephanie Rentel for her excellent artwork, to Martin Walker for his graphics and to Suzie Volpe for her last minute help.

A special thanks to my friends Julia Suzanna Podsiadlo, Sheelagh Rutherford, Judy Malin Onorato, Dale Landry and Stefan Verstappen for all their help.

Once again, I would like to acknowledge all my sisters and brothers, Rose, John, Tony, Ugo, Lorenzo and Lidia for their enthusiasm, moral support and dinners.

Finally, I would like to thank the beautiful little ones, Vanessa, Mariah, Robert and Josette who through their innocent eyes have shown me how to appreciate the simple things in life.

CONTENTS

Forward

By Stefan H. Verstappen

China has been the land of mystery and wonder. Known as Xanadu, Shangri-La, and Cathay, the `Middle Kingdom' is also known for her scientific and magical marvels. Chinese science has given us gunpowder, the compass, the cross-bow, the rudder, and noodles to name a few, while Chinese magic has brought us the I-Ching, Chi Gung, and Feng Shui. Like much that is Chinese, Feng Shui is part science and part magic. While to most westerners the magical aspects of these Chinese arts seem incomprehensible, they all follow the same principles. From acupuncture and herbalism, to Tai Chi and Feng Shui the underlying and common elements concern the flow of energy. This is the cosmological premise of Chinese science, that everything is energy. This energy flows through all creation like rivers and streams flow across the earth and behaves in the same manner as water. Like when a stream runs fast and deep its waters are clear and revitalizing, but where the flow is slow and shallow the water becomes murky and breeds disease.

This is the premise behind Chinese medicine, to restore the flow of blocked energy. If one of the streams of energy that flow through a person's body becomes blocked through an injury, then the energy would stagnate causing disease and eventually poisoning the whole system. Acupuncture is applied to break up the blockages while herbal remedies are aimed at stimulating specific currents of positive energy.

Chi Gung (Internal Energy Skill) seeks to insure the proper flow and increase the production of internal energy through meditation and breathing exercises. Chi is drawn in from the currents of air and directed towards maintaining health and youthfulness.

Tai Chi is also aimed at insuring proper flow of the body's internal energy and directing it outwards to deflect the negative energy from a physical attack. Again the principle strategy of Tai Chi is to behave like water; avoiding what is hard while attacking what is soft.

The philosophy of 'energy is like water' is continued into the art of Feng Shui. The energy being dealt with here is on a larger scale than those found in the body but not much different. It is the energy of the earth, water, colour, shape, alignment, and the deep currents of primordial energy beneath the earth - the dragons. Feng Shui is like adjusting the rabbit ears on a TV to get the best reception. In the world at large the rabbit ears are the elements within a particular environment. By adjusting the various elements in your space, you get a better reception of energy.

The benefit to this unified philosophy is that by mastering one of the arts, you will automatically have an instinctive grasp on the others. Like Confucius wrote. `If I show a student one corner (of a square), I expect him to know there's three more.'

INTRODUCTION

Energy is the basis of all life. It links us to everything in the universe, flowing like a river through our minds, bodies and surroundings. All things in our world are manifestations of energy, and all things are essentially "living". Even though energy moves things, we are unable to observe this phenomenon directly. Everything in our physical world is an expression of energy or Chi, and like a river, the energy within and around us should flow freely and smoothly along its path. When you are in harmony and balance with the energy of your environment this carries over to other aspects of your life creating positive forces and increasing the flow of all good things to you. This concept is at the heart of Feng Shui.

Feng Shui acknowledges the power of the natural world and teaches you to live in harmony with it. The practice of Feng Shui was developed around 618 AD by the Chinese through the interpretation of trigrams found in an ancient divination text called the I Ching or Book of Changes. According to age old Chinese teaching life is based on the movement of Chi and in order to sustains life Chi must keep flowing. To allow this movement to occur there must be something else to move towards. Therefore all things must have at least two primary aspects, Yin and Yang, in order for life to continue to exist.

For this reason Chi is separated into the polarities of Yin and Yang. These two forces create and sustain all life. Yin is feminine, cool and tranquil, it is the forces in the moon, air and water. Yang is masculine, vibrant and hot; it is the force in the sun, thunder and fire, Yin and Yang energies are further intensified and become denser to form the five elements: earth, water, fire, wood and metal from which all things in our physical environment are made. Chi moves in Yin and Yang cycles and through the five elements to bring forth all of creation.

Yin and Yang represent the very essence of life. They symbolize that nothing can exist in and of itself. They are interdependent, forever linked by the relationship each aspect has to each other. Everything exists in relation to everything else. Therefore you cannot change one part of the universe without affecting the entire universe. The dynamic interaction of Yin and Yang forces is affected by the objects with which we surround ourselves, the areas we choose to live in and the degree to which we physically alter our natural environment.

Chi moves in cycles and is continually increasing and decreasing, growing and decaying, flowing quickly or becoming stagnant. The process of change and interaction between Yin and Yang reflects the natural and eternal order known as the way, or the Tao. The Tao speaks of flowing with nature; bending in the face of obstacles and having the wisdom to recognize nature's path in the world around us and as well as within ourselves. Feng Shui is a way of learning to travel in harmonious, natural order with the flow of the Tao.

In fact, affluence comes from the root word affluere, which means, "to flow to". Feng Shui enables you to read your environment and sense the movement and changes within it. By understanding your surroundings and altering the position of certain objects you can create a harmonious environment which will improve your fortunes and enable success, love, prosperity, health and happiness to flow to you in abundance.

CHAPTER ONE

WHAT IS FENG SHUI?

The name Feng Shui (pronounced Fung Shway) is based on two characters, Wind and Water. This ancient art of placement was used to locate the most harmonious surroundings to bury the dead and house the living. Proper site selection would bring luck to the descendants of the buried and would create harmonious conditions for a living space. In traditional Feng Shui, the ideal location was chosen based on the observation of land formations, various earth energies, compass directions and ancient astrological charts. Perfect Feng Shui occurred when a location had lush vegetation, fertile soil, healthy wildlife, and protection from harsh winds as well as an adequate supply of fresh water - hence Feng Shui (Wind Water).

Feng Shui can be traced back to China as early as 618 AD. Core beliefs in Feng Shui were taken from ancient texts that dated as far back as the 4th Century. One such text was called The "Book of

Changes" or the I Ching. This text was filled with predictions, complex language and symbolism, which was difficult to interpret. Feng Shui became a fine art that was limited to the Emperor, his ministers and those who could read. After World War II, China was split in half by communism and Feng Shui was banished along with other feudal practices. Ancient texts were lost, stolen or destroyed and Feng Shui was only practiced in secret. Some of the ancient texts found their way across the water to Taiwan where Feng Shui practices were embraced and utilized both in residential and business spaces. It is no surprise that Taiwan is very rich in industry and trade. Harnessing the earth's natural energies to create harmonious environments was not limited to China and Taiwan. Similar practices were soon discovered in many other parts of the world including India, South American and the Pacific Islands.

TAOISM

Feng Shui is based on philosophical principles of Taoism (pronounced Dowism) also referred to as Tao, "The Way". Chinese Taoism can be dated as far back as the 6th Century BC. The Tao philosophy sees the cycles of nature and constant changes in the natural world as guides and the source of all things in the cosmos. Heaven, earth and every living creature are seen as a whole, connected in an interplay of action and reaction. Tao is to conduct one's life in harmony without disrupting the natural scheme of things.

I CHING

Referred to as The Book of Changes, the I Ching is considered to be one of the oldest texts in the world. The I Ching was formulated over 4000 years ago and includes knowledge and information from many great sages. Chinese ruler Fu His, King Wen of the Chow Dynasty and Confucius were all instrumental in helping to formulate the philosophy behind the I Ching. The text consists of 64 Hexagrams each consisting of a set of three lines that are either broken or solid. A broken line is known as yin and a solid line is known as yang. The lines grouped together to represent Heaven, Man and Earth. It is said that man is influenced by Heaven Luck, Man Luck or Earth Luck. There are eight primary trigrams of the I Ching used in determining life aspirations. Together these symbols form the Pa Kua Grid. Each of the eight trigrams represents one of life's aspirations. When properly interpreted the Pa Kua is a valuable tool used to create good Feng

Shui. The I Ching contains valuable information that has been used to create fortune and good luck to great emperors as well as common folk. Understanding the I Ching in its entirety is a life long study.

APPROACHES

It has been said that there are many approaches to Feng Shui but in fact there are only two original schools of thought, The Form School and The Compass. Most approaches use the basic principles of Form and Compass and add other influences such as religion, cultural beliefs, folklore, superstitions, geomancy, divination, intuition and interior design. Some of the most well known approaches are briefly described below. This book uses the basic form and compass principles together with a common sense approach that is easy to follow and practical to implement. The author respectfully acknowledges that although there are rules and specific calculations involved in Feng Shui cures, intuition and common sense need to be considered when practicing Feng Shui in today's world.

Form School

The form school of thought is based on land

formations. Features of the land were associated with symbolism and given names that became known as the four celestial animals. The most suitable location for a home was in the midst of the Tortoise, Tiger, Phoenix and Dragon. An auspicious location for a home would be sited when the Tortoise feature, a rounded hill was found to the north giving the back of the home protection against the cold winds. The Phoenix to the south would display an outstretched undulating section of land where one could see for miles. In particular a body of water was ideal. The site would need to display a mountainous Dragon feature to the east and a lower rising Tiger feature to the west in order for there to be a well balanced and harmonious living position. Before long locations with good Feng Shui would attract many settlers creating villages and towns. It is interesting to note that ancient burial sites reveal that departed loved ones would be positioned with their head resting in the north. Some tombs even depicted sketches and carvings of the tortoise behind the head of the coffin. There was a strong belief that if the dead where buried in a place with good Feng Shui descendants of the dead would attract good luck for generations.

Compass School

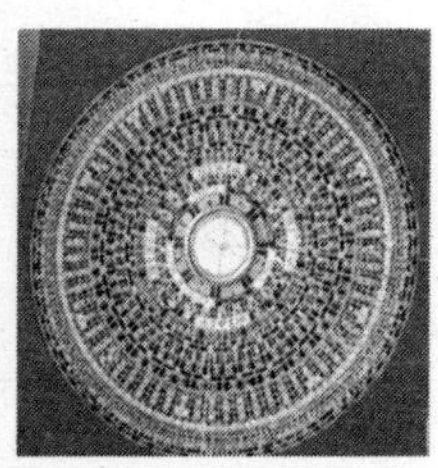

Loupan compass

The compass school of thought based its theories primarily on how a home was situated in relation to the stars in the solar system. A complex compass known as the Loupan was developed to help Practitioners calculate data that would help discern appropriate directions to face a home or furniture. It would also serve as an information system to calculate appropriate time to move, get married, have children and open a business. Feng Shui Masters made their own Loupan and included their own secret formulas. Today only a select few have been privileged to learn the ancient secrets of the great masters. There are only a handful of authentic Masters in the world who use advanced formulas involving the Loupan Compass. These Masters bring with them a deep understanding of ancient Feng Shui practices along with a lifetime of experience. Generally speaking most practitioners today use a simple directional compass.

Flying Star

The Flying Star approach is an exacting art that uses complex formulas to determine date-time-

location calculations that can predict the location and intensity of good or bad energy. Flying Star uses the Lo Shu Square to make calculations. The Lo Shu consists of nine "stars" that move around the square. There can be four stars influencing any one sector of the building at any given time. Time moves in a 20-year luck period. The practitioner gathers and charts information on a building such as date and time it was built and then makes calculations that include the inhabitants' date and time of birth. This is an excellent system to use before construction or extension of a building. Flying Star Masters can detect inauspicious energy before a problem occurs thereby omitting the need to add cures at a later date. Practitioners who have extensive knowledge and experience in authentic Feng Shui formulas should only practice this system.

Black Hat Sect

BHS is one of the most popular approaches in the West. Professor Lin Yun developed this system to reflect western culture. The practice includes the Form school approach along with basic principles such as movement of chi, yin and yang balance, intuition, intention, religion and meditation. One of the major differences is that Black Sect does not use compass direction, however, they do acknowledge it when describing the five-element theory. The Pa Kua grid is referred to as Ba Gua and oriented according to the location of the entrance to a space. Professor Lin Yun started his own BHS Temple in California and has developed a huge following.

Intuitive Feng Shui

Instead of attempting to interpret or calculate complex systems an intuitive practitioner will focus on feelings, instincts and intuitions. This system on its own does not reflect Feng Shui, as there are some basic Feng Shui principles that need to be considered. Most people have the ability to be sensitive to what they feel comfortable with and will make their own decisions based on their own intuitive instinct rather than the instinct of others.

Pyramid School

Nancilee Wydra, founder of the Feng Shui Institute of American and author of several books recently developed this system in the USA. The pyramid school is primarily focused on how place is experienced through the sense of light, colour, smell, sound and touch. The system acknowledges the five element theory but does not consider compass direction. The Pa Kua grid is referred to as the Ba Gua and is oriented according to the front entrance to a room.

Modern Feng Shui

Feng Shui today is a mixture of the above approaches adapted to present day principles. Cultural and religious differences together with climate and location are important considerations of today's modern practitioner.

Form School

*The four celestial animals in an ideal setting:
Tortoise to the north, Pheonix to the south,
Dragon in the east and Tiger in the west creating harmony.*

CHAPTER TWO

THE FLOW

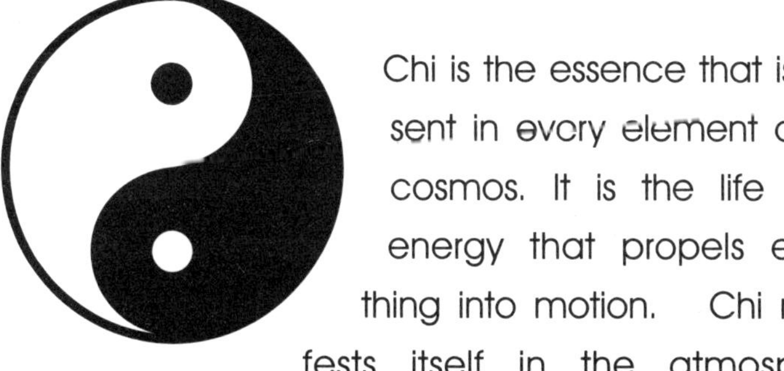

Chi is the essence that is present in every element of the cosmos. It is the life force energy that propels everything into motion. Chi manifests itself in the atmosphere through gentle breezes or powerful winds, and on the earth through land formations such as mountains, hills and valleys. This vital power is inhaled and exhaled, it expands and condenses, it is mass or it can be vapor. When chi enters the depths of the earth and expands, it can erupt as in an active volcano, which is similar to a person consuming contaminated food and vomiting. In order for people to be healthy and prosperous the chi must be balanced and flow freely.

The Chinese have utilized the principles of chi for thousands of years. Martial artists demonstrate the power of chi via the powerful strike of a single hand movement. Acupuncturists use needles to tap into the body's meridian to unblock and balance chi.

If chi could be observed by the naked eye it would look like water moving in a stream or river. The ideal condition would be for the water to be gently meandering. Large rocks and excess debris in the water interrupt the flow and force erratic conditions. A straight path would cause the water to move quickly and rapidly to its destination. Water that is stuck in one spot with nowhere to go would eventually become stale and stagnate, creating a lifeless and noxious condition known as Sha Chi.

Recognizing and utilizing the positive flow of chi in an environment is a vital component of Feng Shui. A trained eye can tune in to and harness the natural pulses of the earth and stay clear of the negative energies that can cause ill effects.

Some of the factors that affect the flow of chi of an environment are as follows:

Vegetation

Healthy vegetation is the first and most important indicator of a location with good Feng Shui. Natural vegetation must be observed when considering a site on which to build. Dead or decayed branches on a tree can be a sign that the tree is diseased or has been affected by either wildlife or the weather. Stagnant water in the area contains harmful chemicals that destroy vegetation. Certain trees attract butterflies while others attract annoying insects such as mosquitoes. An awareness of the condition and type of vegetation may help select a sight that will bring positive chi into and around your home.

Pathways

A pathway can be defined as that which gets you from one point to another. The road that takes you to your destination will set feelings and attitudes into motion long before you arrive. Sidewalks, roads, driveways, footpaths, entranceways and hallways are all passages that lead you from one experience to another. The energy you feel during the journey will depend on whether the pathway is long and narrow, bright and cheerful or bumpy and crowded. Consider the most relaxing path you ever walked upon and the most nerve-racking plane ride you have taken.

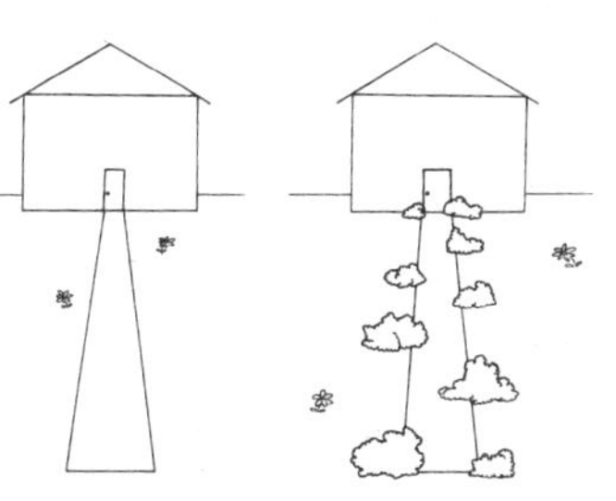

Placement of Furniture and Objects

How and where objects are placed in a space can have a profound effect on the inhabitants of the space. Furniture placed too closely together creates the same feeling as a crowded elevator - stuffy with no air to breathe. Furniture should always be placed in such a way that it is easy to navigate. As a rule sofas, chairs and beds should always have an unimpaired view of the doorway. Paintings and other objects should be carefully analyzed as to their meaning before being displayed in key locations. A painting of a violent storm with waves crashing against the rocks may cause restless sleep, if located on a bedroom wall.

Maintenance

Keeping a home and its contents in good repair and in working order is a reflection of how you feel about yourself. Uncut grass, overgrown weeds and dead plants around your home give the impression of abandonment and neglect. Cracked driveways, walkways and windows catch Sha chi between the cracks creating a sense of old age and staleness. A leaky faucet could mean your wealth is going down the drain. Broken appliances, objects and furniture attract negative energy and should either be fixed or thrown out.

Clutter

Everything is attached to you with a constantly tugging string. Clutter is one of the main causes of stale energy in and around a home. When chi enters your home it can get stuck in crowded corners, over-stuffed closets, over-filled drawers or on messy counter tops. A good rule to follow is if you don't like it, don't need it or haven't used it in two years, get rid of it. Clearing clutter is one of the first and most important steps in practicing successful Feng Shui.

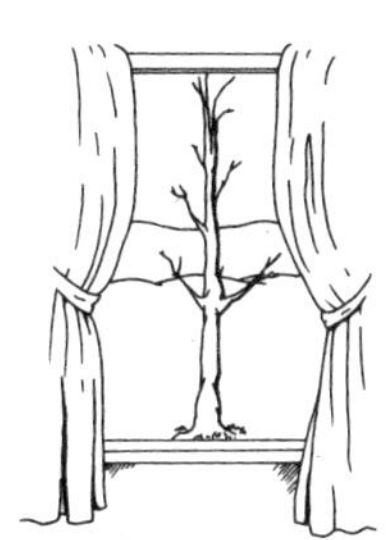

Poison Arrows

A poison arrow is like the cutting edge of a blade - pointed in your direction. A poison arrow can be a tall hydro pole located directly in front of your doorway, greeting you each day as you step outside, or a tall building looming over your home. Beams across a ceiling that create a heavy oppressed feeling can also be considered poison arrows. When two sharp edges meet they cause negative energy and are also considered poison arrows.

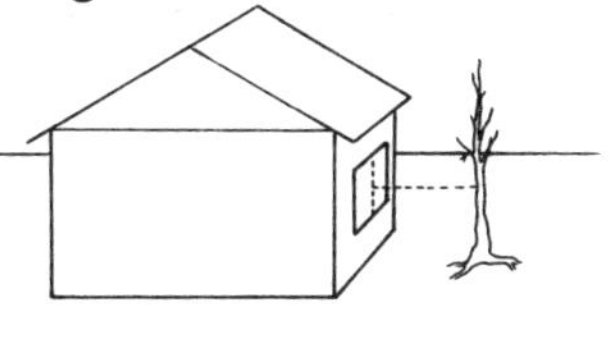

Blocks

In Feng Shui a block is that which stops or interrupts the flow of chi. If a tree or branch fell across your driveway then its removal would be necessary. Overgrown trees blocking the view from a window or masking the entrance to your home are examples of blocks. Inside your home, excessive or oversized furniture in a small room can impede or smother the flow of chi.

Electromagnetic Fields

The subtle energy given off by overhead power lines, transformer boxes, electric blankets, small appliances, televisions and computers is a proven health risk with long periods of exposure. Although it is difficult to avoid using modern appliances such as blow dryers or computers it is important to realize that all of these create magnetic fields that can affect your well being. Electromagnetic fields cannot be seen by the naked eye, however, as indicated by car radio static and interference, they are always surrounding us.

Yin and Yang Balance

In Feng Shui the concept of yin and yang are terms to describe the flow of chi in the universe. Taoist tradition teaches that all things in the cosmos are based on two opposing yet complimentary principles called yin and yang. These forces contain a little of each in the other and are intertwined in a constant cyclic dance creating harmony and balance in all things. Yin is dark and still, while yang is light and in motion. The movement of planetary systems and the brightness of stars and suns balance the darkness of the universe. On earth daylight is yang while nighttime is yin. This system of opposites in harmony is used to evaluate the flow of energy in an environment. Traditional Feng Shui based land formations on the yin and yang systems. A tall mountain was yang while a deep valley was yin. A place is balanced and has good Feng Shui when it is neither boring nor agitating but promotes the right level of energy for the business at hand. Neither yin nor yang is ever 100% pure - one always contains a little of the other. All things contain varying degrees of yin and yang but a balance is most beneficial. Characteristics of yin and yang are listed on the following page.

YIN	YANG
Dark	Light
Inward	Outward
Curved	Straight
Moon	Sun
Night	Day
Female	Male
Passive	Active
Cold	Hot
Death	Life
Low	High
Receptive	Projective

COLOURS

Black	White
Beige	Yellow
Soft Pink	Red

SCENTS

Lilac	Lemon
Lavender	Eucalyptus
Rose	Mint

SOUND

Rustling Leaves	Lawn Mower
Babbling Brook	Niagara Falls
Whispering	Shouting
Ticking Watch	Cookoo Clock

PATTERNS

Curved and wavy	Sharp and straight
Circles	Pyramids
Semi circle	Criss Cross

TASTE

Sweet	Spicy
Creamy	Crunchy

CHAPTER THREE

THE FIVE ELEMENTS

The Five-Element Theory is an elegant system derived by the Taoists as a way of understanding the interacting phases of chi energy. The five elements represent everything in the universe that is visible and invisible. Based on observation, the Chinese concluded that the entire universe is based on cycles and rhythms of yin and yang chi energy affecting each other in a play of creation, reduction and domination. Our world begins each day with the sun rising in the east and ends with it setting in the west. The year begins with the cold winter giving way to the spring then summer followed by the fall and then winter again. Like yin/yang and chi, the Five Element Theory is an important principle of good Feng Shui. The elements are Wood, Fire, Earth, Metal and Water. Each one of these is associated with compass direction, colours, shapes, seasons, feelings and characteristics. Landscapes, buildings, rooms, doors and people can be characterized by the five elements. Based on their year of birth each person possesses a dominant element that can be used to analyze personal energy as well as the energy of the environment. The creative cycle of the elements represents harmony and balance. When the elements are off balance the dominant or reduction cycle is used to make adjustments. Compass direction and colour is the best way to add, enhance or change the energy of a space. When this is not possible the elements shape can be used.

Each of the doors below represents one of the five elements, earth, fire, metal wood and water. The energy of an element can easily be introduced to an area or object by using shapes or patterns.

WOOD

COLOUR	*Green*
DIRECTION	*East*
SEASON	*Spring*
TIME OF DAY	*Dawn*
SHAPE	*Rectangle*
SYMBOL	*Dragon*
CHARACTERISTIC	*Nourishment, upward growth, creativity, renewal, change, ideas*
FEELINGS	*Fresh, happy, active, hope, adventurous*
BUILDINGS	*Tall, rectangular, skyscrapers and towers, healing centers, restaurants and hospitals*
ROOMS	*Children's bedrooms, kitchen and dining room*
OBJECTS	*Trees, plants, flowers, wooden frames, books, newspapers, organic fibers such as linen or cotton*

FIRE

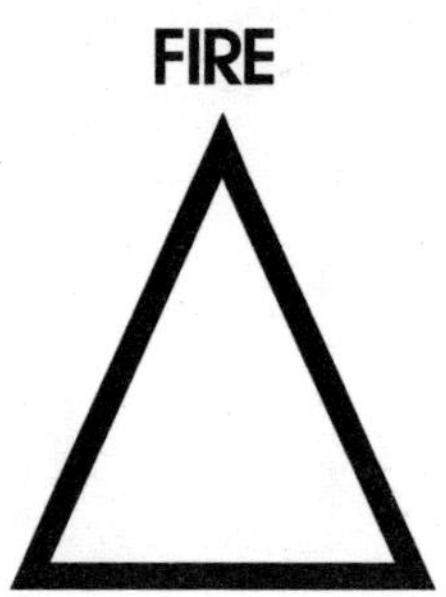

COLOUR	*Red and Purple*
DIRECTION	*South*
SEASON	*Summer*
TIME OF DAY	*High noon*
SHAPE	*Triangle*
SYMBOL	*Phoenix*
CHARACTERISTIC	*Action, activity, agitation, power, attention, danger.*
FEELINGS	*Enthusiasm, hot, energy and excitement*
BUILDINGS	*Pointed and angled roofs, churches, casinos, dance-halls, libraries, schools, vet clinics, high fashion industry*
ROOMS	*Game rooms, ceremonial rooms*
OBJECTS	*Candles, light bulbs, fire, leather*

EARTH

COLOUR	*Terra cotta, brown, yellow and all earth tones.*
DIRECTION	*Centre and southwest*
SEASON	*Late summer*
TIME OF DAY	*Mid afternoon*
SHAPE	*Square*
SYMBOL	*Earth*
CHARACTERISTIC	*Solid, even, stable and grounded*
FEELINGS	*Comfortable, safe and secure*
BUILDINGS	*Low, square, brick and concrete, Hospitals, courthouses, jails, museums, retirement homes and storage buildings*
ROOMS	*Sitting room, storage room, garage and conservatories*
OBJECTS	*Bricks, clay, concrete, sand and rocks*

METAL

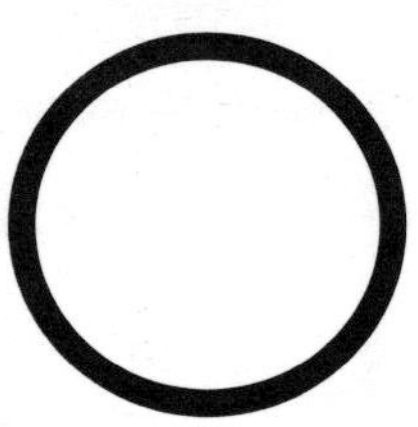

COLOUR	*White, silver, grey and gold*
DIRECTION	*West*
SEASON	*Autumn*
TIME OF DAY	*Dusk*
SHAPE	*Round, oval or domed*
SYMBOL	*White tiger*
CHARACTERISTIC.	*Sharp, refined, precise.*
FEELINGS	*Focused, intense concentration, clear and moral*
BUILDINGS	*Domed, curved roofs, reflective and shiny buildings, civic and financial institutions, observatories, hardware stores, jewelers, computer stores, banks*
ROOMS	*Kitchen, bathroom and workshop*
OBJECTS	*Metal, gold and steel coins and medals, mirrors, wires, wind chimes and aluminum*

WATER

COLOUR	*Blue and black*
DIRECTION	*North*
SEASON	*Winter*
TIME OF DAY	*Midnight*
SHAPE	*Undulating*
SYMBOL	*Turtle*
CHARACTERISTIC	*Yielding, transmission of ideas, comfortable, easy,*
FEELINGS	*social interaction, wisdom Relaxed, easy going, clear thinking*
BUILDINGS	*Nurseries, travel agencies, aquariums,radio and television*
ROOMS	*Laundry, bathroom, hospital rooms, treatment rooms*
OBJECTS	*Fish bowls, running water, fountains, glass, plastics and ice*

The five elements interact with each other in three different cyles. The first is the Cyle of creation, the next is the cycle of reduction and the last is the cycle of domination. The creative cycle is the natural flow of energy.

CYCLE OF CREATION

Water grows and nourishes wood
Wood creates and feeds fire
Fire burns and makes earth
Earth particles make metal
Metal attracts and holds water

THE CYCLE OF REDUCTION

Water reduces metal by rusting
Metal reduces earth by condensing
Earth smothers fire
Fire burns and consumes wood
Wood absorbs water

THE CYCLE OF DOMINATION

Earth stops water
Water puts out fire
Fire melts metal
Metal chops wood
Wood consumes earth

THE FIVE ELEMENTS AND THEIR CHARACTERISTICS
Easy Reference Chart

ELEMENT	DIRECTION	COLOUR	SHAPE	EXPRESSES	OBJECTS
WOOD	East	Green	Rectangle	Growth, Nourishment, Creativity	Plants,Flowers, Trees
FIRE	South	Red	Triangle	Action, Energy, Danger, Power	Stove, Furnace, Candles, Stop Sign
EARTH	NW,SE Centre	Brown, Beige	Square	Stability, Reliability, Safety	Earth, Stones, Bricks, Clay Pots
METAL	West	White Reflective	Round	Reflection, Restraint, Precision	Coins, Swords, Windchimes, Mirror
WATER	North	Blue, Black	Curved Undulating	Easygoing, Mystery, Communications	Fish Tanks, Fountains, Ponds, Glass

CHAPTER FOUR

THE PA KUA

The Pa Kua is a term used to describe an octagon shaped grid that is used in Feng Shui to help determine flow and balance within a space. The grid is divided in eight sections that are characterized by sets of trigrams containing a combination of either yang (solid) or yin (broken) lines. Each trigram is assigned a name, number, element, colour, compass direction and life aspiration. The grid (below) is a

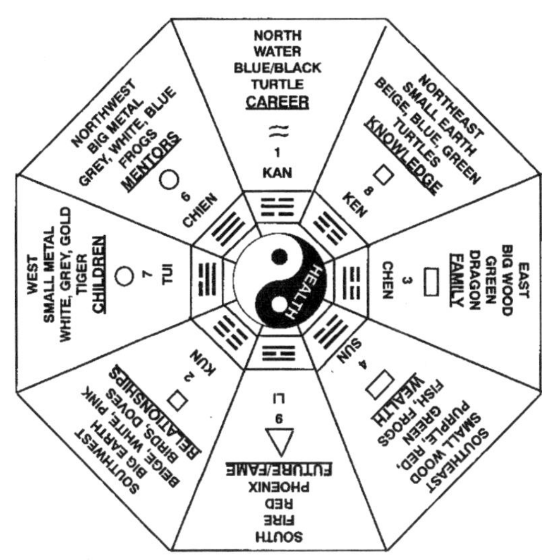

valuable tool that can be used to make decisions, solve problems and create harmony within any given space.

There are a number of ways in which the Pa Kua can be oriented over a space. One popular method is by orienting the grid according to the front door. The career, knowledge or mentor area would fall over your front entrance depending on which third of the wall the door is on. With this method the wealth area would always fall in the top left corner of the space. As a result, depending on the location of the door the wealth may fall in different locations of any given room. However by orienting the grid by using the compass the wealth area will always fall into the southeast area of a space, regardless of the front door location.

In this book we use the compass method to orient the Pa Kua. The compass method has traditionally been used for thousands of years and is known to be highly effective. It may be a little confusing at first but with a little practice and patience the results will be worthwhile.

You will need to construct a floor plan showing shape and compass orientation. You will need a simple compass, a pencil, paper and a ruler. To determine which direction your home faces hold the compass in front of you, stand inside your front door and look outside. The direction you are facing is the facing direction of your home. The front door is the door that denotes the face of your home.

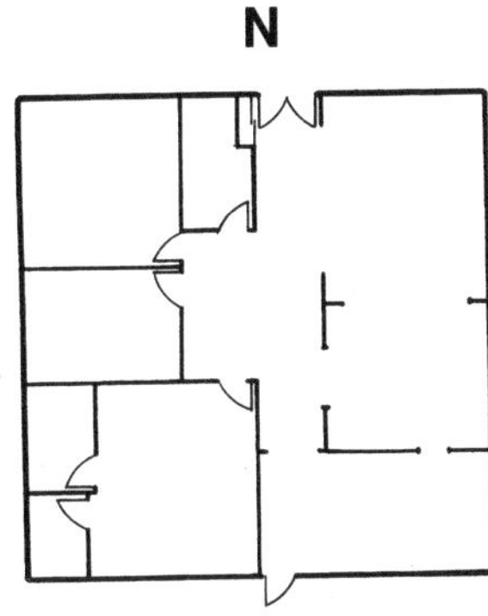

Once you have a reading and have found the magnetic direction you can place the grid over your floor plan simply by matching the compass direction with the direction of your home. Although there is a difference in degrees between the true compass direction and the magnetic compass direction we suggest you use the magnetic method for simplicity sake.

The eight sections of the Pa Kua are evenly divided into 45 degree sections. Note that the magnetic compass direction is located in the centre of the associated trigram. Example - magnetic north falls in the centre of the Kun/career trigram.

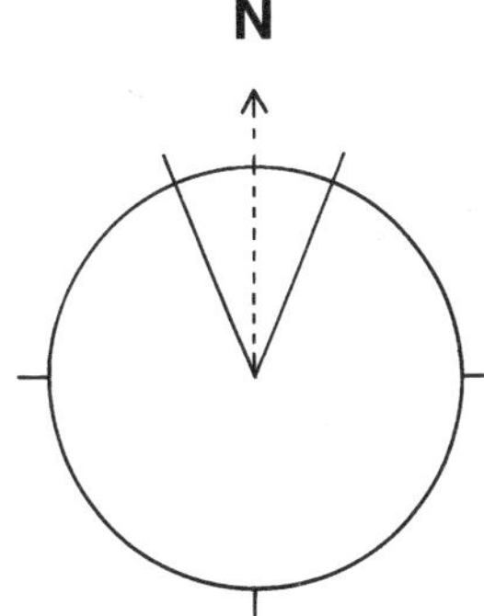

The Pa Kua can be placed over your entire space to locate which trigram falls into what room and then can be placed over each individual room to identify each section of the room itself.

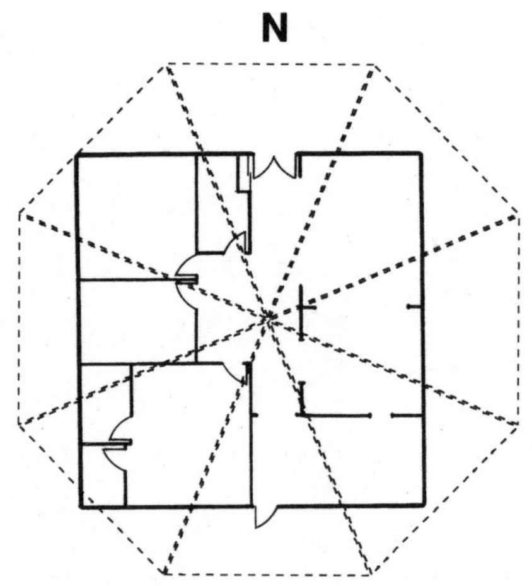

Once you learn how to orient the grid you can begin to analyze your space. Since each of the trigrams is associated with a compass direction, colour and element you can begin to create balance by making sure that each area is in harmony with it's associated element. Example. if your front door is facing south, be sure it is green or red. If you find that you have a spare room located in the northern section of your home paint it blue or gray and use it for your office. The Pa Kua can also be a valuable tool when moving into a new home it can help you select the best place for an office or bedroom.

Pa Kua can help you activate areas of your life by helping to analyze and balance your space, select auspicious colour schemes and place items in any area that will help activate your life aspirations.

PERSONAL KUA

The Kua number is system that helps to identify your most and least favourable compass directions. Kua is based on your birth year and is different for male and females. Each number relates to one of the eight trigrams, each possessing it's own element and compass direction. First look up your Kua number by referring to the chart at the end of this chapter. Those born in either January or February should first check the lunar chart on page 87 to determine the beginning of your birth year.

In Feng Shui the number five is traditionally associated with the centre of the Pa Kua and although it is considered an essential position it does not have its own particular forecast. Females who calculate their number as five should use eight and males use two.

The following chart lists the most favourable

and least favourable directions for each Kua number. There are four favourable and unfavourable directions for every person. Remember, it is only a guide to the fortune of the direction you are assessing, therefore they should be interpreted in relation to your character and circumstances. In other words, if your Kua number is two and your bed is facing North but you have no difficulty sleeping then it is not necessary to make any changes. Keep in mind, that there are ways to improve your unfavourable directions.

The Chinese have given a name and a definition for each auspicious and inauspicious area. Familiarize yourself with each area and it's implied meaning. Once you understand this section refer to the chart on the next page to determine which compass directions are best for you and which directions should be avoided.

Each location has been given a Key. For example auspicious directions are from G1 to G4 and inauspicious are identified as B1 to B4.

PERSONAL KUA #	1	2	3	4	6	7	8	9
DIRECTION								
North	G4	B4	G2	G1	B3	B1	B2	G3
Northeast	B2	G1	B3	B4	G2	G3	G4	B1
East	G2	B1	G4	G3	B2	B4	B3	G1
Southeast	G1	B2	G3	G4	B1	B3	B4	G2
South	G3	B3	G1	G2	B4	B2	B1	G4
Southwest	B4	G4	B1	B2	G3	G2	G1	B3
West	B1	G2	B4	B3	G1	G4	G3	B2
Northwest	B3	G3	B2	B1	G4	G1	G2	B4

AUSPICIOUS LOCATIONS

G1 Sheng Chi location is great for attracting wealth and is best for front door, bedroom, den or home office.

G2 Tien Yi is the best area for good health and uplifting energy. A wood burning stove, furnace room or kitchen is great in this area.

G3 Nien Yen is the best area to encourage healthy family relationships. Master Bedrooms, children's bedroom, the nursery, dining room and family rooms are best located in this area.

G4 Fu Wei area is considered to be an area where overall balance, harmony and tranquility can be achieved. Locate the family room or living room or dining room in this area.

INAUSPICIOUS LOCATIONS

B1 Ho Hai can mean financial losses, general hardship. Good for a storage room.

B2 Wu Kwei is associated with loss of Income, fires, burglary and quarrels and misunderstandings with family. A toilet is good for this area.

B3 Lui Sha implies missed opportunities with work and can cause legal problems, illness and accidents. Toilets or storage rooms are best in this area.

B4 Chueh Ming is the worst of all locations. It can

mean total loss including family, friends and money. Avoid a home with the front door in this location. A toilet or kitchen would be good in this area.

Try to sit facing your most auspicious areas. If this is not possible try to avoid B3 or B4.

When sleeping try to locate your bed so that your head is resting in your most auspicious area. Toilets are best located in the B areas particularly in the B4 area.

Use the productive cycle of the elements to enhance your own personal Kua. For example, if your Kua number is 4, you are wood and wood is fed by water so therefore blue would be a lucky colour for you. If your Kua is 9 your element is fire therefore wood feeds fire and your lucky colour would be green.

CHAPTER FIVE

CURES AND TIPS

LIGHT

The amount of light in your surroundings has a profound affect on health and emotions. Lack of sunlight can create feelings of depression whereas sunlight energizes and uplifts. To add yang to a space use brighter lighting or light pointed upward. To add yin use low or dim lighting that is focussed downward.

- ☯ Increase lighting by replacing bulbs with higher wattage or use full spectrum bulbs.
- ☯ Lamps and spotlights can be used to highlight objects and plants creating a different dimension.
- ☯ Diversion can be created by pointing a lamp or spotlight over a shiny object on a table or counter.
- ☯ Crystal prisms hung in front of a window disperse white light as a rainbow of colours.
- ☯ Position a mirror across from a window to bring

more light into a room.

☯ Add light to a windowless room by highlighting a scenic picture with a light and then placing a mirror on the wall facing it.

COLOUR

Studies from around the world indicate that colours directly affect they way we feel. In a recent study, prison cells painted bubble gum pink resulted in less agitated prisoners. The colour red is a high energy colour that can be used to elevate moods and attract attention such as with stop signs or traffic lights. Colour is also used to create a desired effect in a room.

☯ When selecting colours use the creative cycle of the five elements to create balance. Wood (green) to fire (red, pink, peach) to earth (brown, beige, yellow) to metal (white, gray or reflective) to water (blue, navy or black). By using tints and tones of the primary colours, harmony and balance can easily be achieved. A colour scheme for a living room may look like this:

1. Green carpet, peach walls and beige ceiling (wood-fire-earth)
2. Red carpet, beige walls and white ceiling (fire-earth-metal)

3. Silver carpet, blue walls and green ceiling (metal-water-wood)

To achieve perfect harmony accent the room with the missing elements:

1. Gray and black accents (metal and water)
2. Blue or black and green (water and wood)
3. Red and brown (fire and earth)

☯ The best colour to use for the front door is the colour that feeds the direction. If your front door faces east (wood/green) the best colour to use would be blue/black (water/north) because water feeds wood and gives it energy.

SOUND

By definition sound is a vibration that causes a sensation in the ear experienced as noise or sound depending on the recipients' interpretation. A teenager's music may be noise to an adult whereas teens would find an adult's music annoying. Sound is an important part of Feng Shui and should be included as part of a harmonious environment in your

home. Whether you are living alone or with a large family the introduction of sound can encourage positive energy in any space.

☯ Windchimes create a gentle tinkling sound when the wind brushes against them. Hang a windchime outside a door or close to a window. Hollow tubes on metal windchimes are the most auspicious.

☯ Place leafy plants near slightly open windows to encourage the rustling of the leaves.

☯ Use automatic timers to turn music on at regular intervals.

☯ Put a bird bath or bird house outside windows to attract singing birds.

SMELL

The nose is never asleep. When the sense of smell meets freshly baked bread or cotton candy our memory evokes past experiences like Mom's home baking or the trip to the Exhibition. With the popularity of aromatherapy dozens of fragrances and scents can be introduced into an environment to create a number of desired effects. There are scents that can relax, uplift and relieve stress. All of these can be introduced by incense, candles, sprays, oils and small ceramic pots.

- Manderin or orange scent can be used by the door to help create a comfortable relaxed feeling.
- Lemon or pine can be used in areas where energy needs uplifting.

SYMBOLS

Chinese culture is very rich in symbolism. Symbols are often used as cures. One of the most popular is the bamboo flutes. They represent peace, tranquility and contentment. They can be hung over a door to bring in good luck or hung on a beam in pairs to disperse oppressive energy. They are best hung by red thread with the mouthpiece facing downward. Other good luck objects include the three legged frog, the lucky cat piggy bank and a variety of chinese coins.

- Use your own lucky symbols to attract luck. In the west a lucky rabbits foot, a horseshoe or four leaf clover are common symbols for luck.
- Symbols of spiritual pictures and statues can be wonderful Feng Shui cures. Create feelings of peace by placing framed pictures of saints, angels or spirit guides. These symbols are best placed in the Mentor area. See the Pa Kua for

details.

☯ Outdoors, heavy statues such as lions and gargoyles can be used to symbolically guard the home against intruders. It is best to display less aggressive animals indoors.

☯ Heavy statues or clay pots represent solid stable grounds and can be used to provide feelings of security or to draw attention away from an undesirable object.

LIFE

Life can be added to home in the form of animals or plants. Studies have proven that caring for a plant or pet can be both rewarding and healthy. Life adds yang energy to a yin space. Those living alone can benefit from life energy.

☯ Domestic pets such as birds, cats and dogs add life to a home.

☯ Birdhouses and baths placed outdoors will attract chirping birds. There are a variety of plants and trees that can be used to attract colourful butterflies.

☯ Chinese money plant or jade is considered lucky, especially in the wealth area.

☯ A hanging planter in a window can cover up an undesirable scene.

- Cut flowers add colour and energy to a space.
- Avoid using dried flowers. They do not add life to a room, however synthetic flowers and plants are acceptable.
- Uplift energy and add the sense of smell by using fragrant flowers.
- Plants and flowers help to soften the effects of sharp edges in a room.

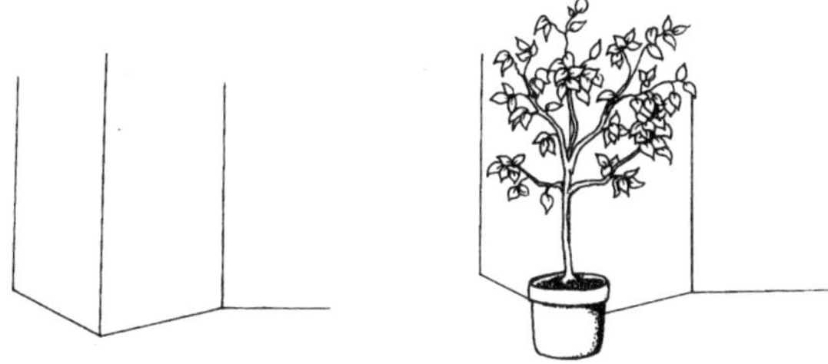

MOVEMENT

Movement is an ideal way to introduce life into a still area. Movement summons attention and is good as a distraction. Wind-sensitive objects include flags, banners, mobiles, windmills and fans are ideal.

- Point a fan to a leafy tree to create movement and the soothing sound of rustling leaves. The same fan can be pointed at a curtain or a mobile.

- An aquarium or fish bowl

with live fish is soothing to look at and at the same time adds movement and life to a still space.

☯ Mobiles, wind chimes and wind socks are excellent for breaking up and dispersing negative shars or poison arrows.

WATER

Water is considered to be very lucky in Feng Shui. Life on earth cannot be sustained without it. Having this element present in a home can encourage and uplift energy. Water represents wealth and prosperity in traditional Feng Shui.

☯ Tabletop fountains, aquariums and fish bowls are excellent ways of bringing water into a home.

☯ The trickling sound of an indoor water fountain or aquarium is soothing and relaxing.

☯ Water fountains are visually pleasing and add an uplifting moisture to the air.

☯ Water features in the north enhance the energy of that direction. Doing this would also enhance your career prospects.

☯ Adding a small fountain or fish bowl with gold fish in the southeast corner of a home or office is said to be auspicous for attracting wealth.

MIRRORS

Mirrors are great cures in Feng Shui. They can be used for many different purposes including expanding a space, bringing in light, making a space disappear and reflecting a beautiful scene.

- ☯ Do not hang a mirror in a position where it cuts off people's heads.
- ☯ Place a mirror across from a dining area to double the quantity of food.
- ☯ Placing a mirror in a confined area can make it appear larger, such as the inside of an elevator.
- ☯ Placing a mirror on a protruding beam can make it disappear.
- ☯ Avoid tiled mirrors on walls as they break up your image.

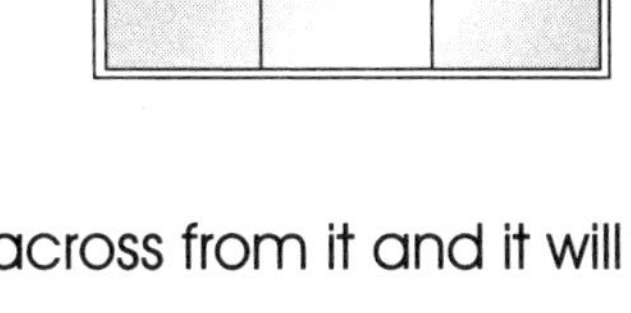

- ☯ Replace all cracked or chipped mirrors.
- ☯ When a room has only one window, hang a mirror directly across from it and it will appear like there are two windows in the room.
- ☯ Never sleep with a mirror facing you as it will create ill feelings. When this cannot be avoided place a plant or scarf in front of mirror.

TIPS

Buying, Building, or Renting

• Research. Who were the previous owners? Why did they move? When was the building erected? What occupied the space or land before the building went up?

☯ Check out the condition of the vegetation. Are the large trees diseased or damaged? What types of trees, shrubs and flowers surround the home or building? Some trees attract butterflies while others attract annoying insects.

☯ Check compass direction to determine where the sun hits at different times of the day . Will the sun shine on the garden? Is your home protected from the cold damaging winds?

☯ Check if the building is higher than others. Looming buildings may cause Inferior feelings.

☯ Does the *driveway slope* down or is it elevated? A driveway that slopes down may be lead to flooding of the basement. It is best to climb up rather than to step down.

☯ Is there a body of *water* nearby and if so what life does it support? Stagnant water often contains chemicals that kill vegetation and attract unappealing insect life.

☯ *Check below ground level* for abnormalities such

as a clay bottom or high water table that could make building a home unsuitable or costly.

☯ Check for *high voltage generators* or *hydro lines* that emit strong electromagnetic waves. Be sure that they are within a safe distance.

☯ Avoid *spaces that look onto cemetaries or factories*

PATHWAYS AND ROADWAYS

☯ Pathways leading to your home should be kept in good condition. Pot holes, cracks and a broken sidewalks are an indication of a life in disrepair. Repairing the main roads and sidewalks is the responsibility of the government so you and your neighbors should not hesitate in voicing your concern. First impressions are the most important so keep driveways and pathways in good shape.

☯ Plant flowers and plants alongside the pathway leading to the door. Curve a narrow straight pathway by using plants, bushes, shrubs or lights on either side.

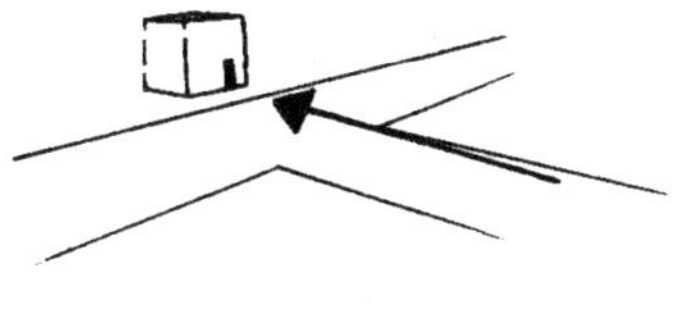

Do not arrange them so that they are directly across from each other.

FRONT ENTRANCES

- Entrances one of the most important areas of a space. They should be welcoming and easy to see from the road. Draw attention to the door by adding bright lights or wind chimes.The front entrance is an indication of what lies inside. It tells everyone how you feel about your home and yourself. If the entrance is dark and gloomy, the impression will be the same.
- Keep front entrances in good repair. Ensure that there is no peeling paint or cracks in the door. Be sure the door does not squeak and closes properly.
- The door should be in proper proportion to the size of the home or building. Large double doors are well suited to large homes where a single well-manicured door looks lovely on a small townhouse.
- Townhouse or apartment doors can be distinguished from the others by hanging plants, door ornaments or by placing a doormat on the threshold.
- Doors should open wide and feel welcoming . When doors don't open completely it gives the impression that there is something to hide.

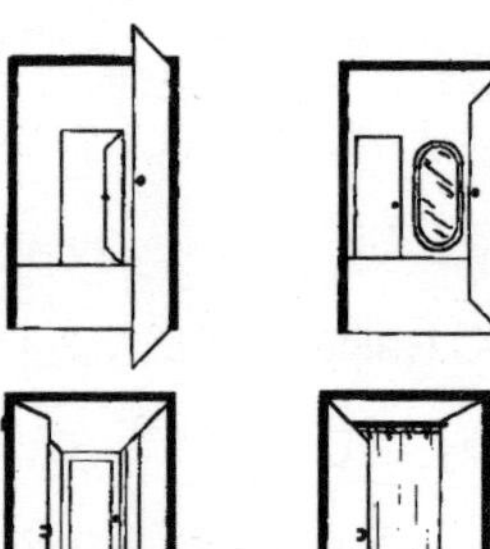

- A door opening into or facing another door or window creates a straight fast moving path. Redirect the flow by creating diversions that will slow down or attract the energy towards the main gathering area of the home.

STAIRWAYS

- Front doors that open to face the stairs create a straight path of energy. Occupants may want to spend most of their time upstairs. Redirect the flow of energy by creating a diversion by placing objects and items that pull the energy towards another area of the space.

- Stairs with open backs are inauspicious. If they cannot be covered place large plants or heavy objects under the staircase.
- Spiral staircases can be compared to a corkscrew that drills and burrows into the space. Avoid a staircase in the middle of a home. Avoid red carpeting on spiral stairs.
- Curved and gently winding staircases are the most auspicious.
- Hang pictures or mirrors on the walls of long narrow staircases.

WINDOWS

☯ Windows are considered the eyes of a home and should be kept in good repair. Replace all broken or cracked windows and keep them clean and free of clutter.

☯ Windows are the eyes of the home and should have a pleasant view. A window that looks out at a unpleasant scene such as a cemetary, brick wall or busy highway creates negative energy. Cover the window with an appropriate window dressing, screen or plant.

CEILINGS

☯ Ceilings are the sky of a room and should be painted in a light airy colour. If the ceiling is too high,

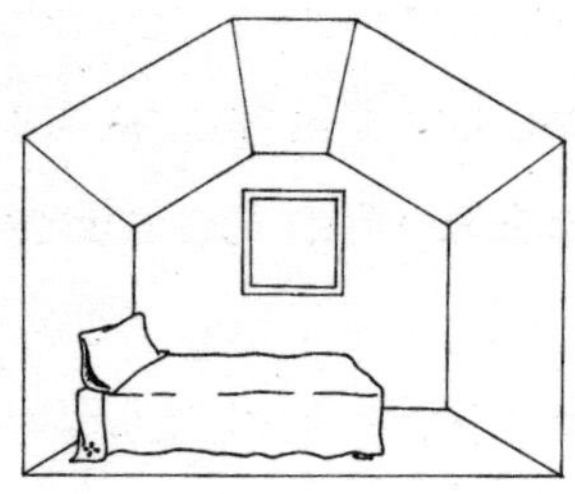

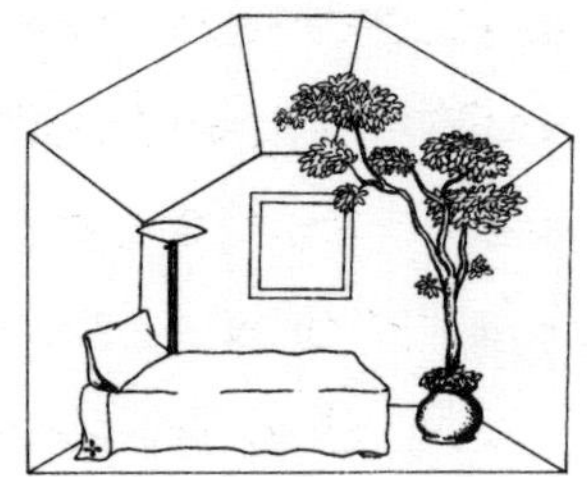

using a darker shade can bring it down.

☯ Beams on low ceilings create an oppressive feeling and should be as inconspicuous as possible. Paint them the same colour as the ceiling or defuse their affects by decorating with vines, lights or

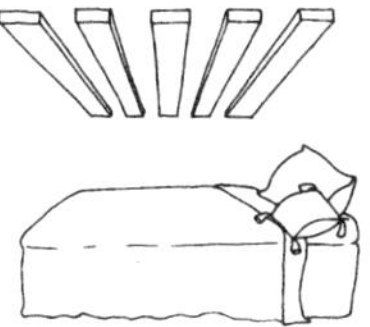

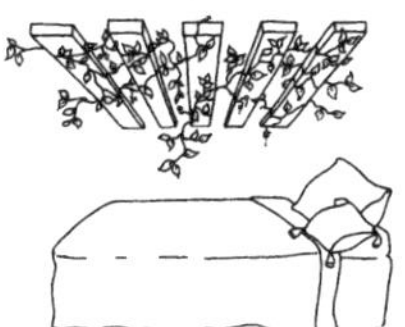

mobiles.

☯ Do not place a sofa, bed or chair under a beam. Place shiny objects and brighter lights at eye level to distract attention away from the ceiling. When beds cannot be moved place tall plants or upward facing lights in the room to uplift the energy.

BATHROOMS

☯ Bathroom doors should always be kept closed, especially if the bathroom is located close to an entrance or near a gathering area.

☯ Toilet seats should be kept down at all times as it is believed that all the chi energy will be flushed away down the drains.

☯ Avoid dried flowers or stale pot pourri. Fresh or synthetic flowers are best.

☯ When a bathroom door faces a main seating or sleeping area paint it the same colour as the wall and put up pictures or place heavy objects on the side of the door to create a diversion.

☯ When space permits place a screen or wall separating the toilet from the bathtub.

- Bright lights and mirrors are auspicious in bathrooms.
- Good colours for bathrooms are white, green, blue or beige.

KITCHEN

- Kitchen area or fridge clearly visible from the front door may cause overeating. Keep the lights closed when not in use or use sound, objects, mobiles to lure the attention to another area.
- Stoves are the most important part of the kitchen and should be kept clean and in good repair. Be sure all of the cooking elements are functioning.
- The cook's back should not be to the door. Place a small mirror at the side or above the stove so that the door can be seen at all times.
- Auspicious colours for sinks are metal, black or white. Avoid the colour red for a sink.
- Good colours for a kitchen are white, green, blue or cream.

DINING ROOM

- Oval or round tables are best as they allow the chi to flow all around.
- The table should be brightly lit by a ceiling light or

chandelier.

- Avoid beams over the table.
- The table should be located in the centre of a room.
- A mirror reflecting the table is auspicious as it doubles the food.
- Good colors for the dining area are white, green and orange.

LIVING ROOM/GATHERING AREA

- Sofas and chairs should be arranged to face each other to encourage conversation.
- Backs should not be to the door. Sofas and chairs should have their backs to the wall.
- Allow sufficient room around each piece of furniture to create better flow.
- Televisions should never be the center of attraction in a gathering area.
- Never put the television in the power area of the room (the area of a room that is the furthest from the door and has the clearest view of the entire room.)

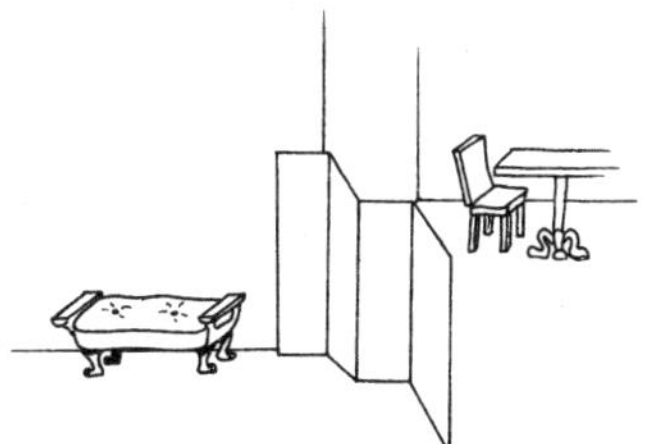

- Large L shaped living room/dining room spaces can be separated by using plants or screens. Area carpets and ceiling boarders are also effective.

BEDROOMS

- ☯ Bedrooms are for rest and relaxation. Avoid placing exercise machines, televisions and ironing boards within view of your sleeping position.
- ☯ Headboard should be well-fastened and against a solid wall.
- ☯ Position beds so that you have a clear view of the room's entrance.
- ☯ Avoid positions where your bed is directly lined up

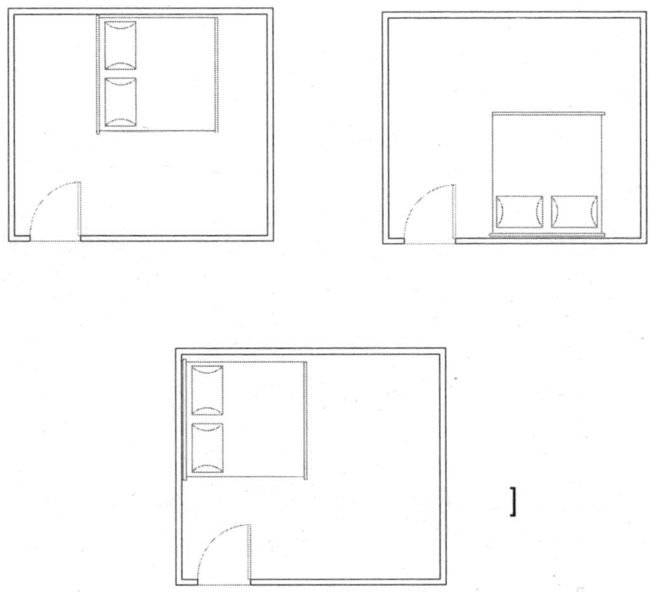

The above bed positions are inauspicous

Position beds so that the door can be clearly seen from where you lay your head

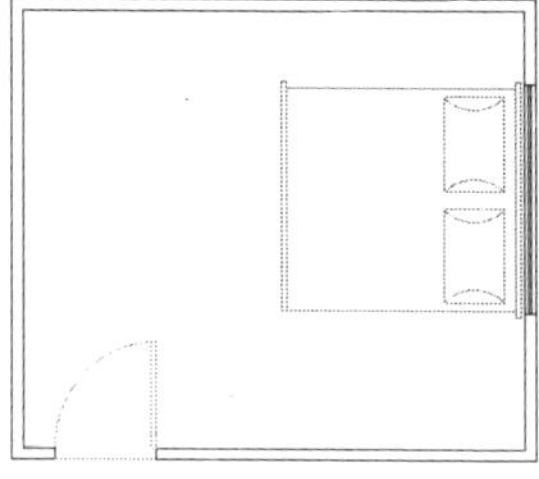

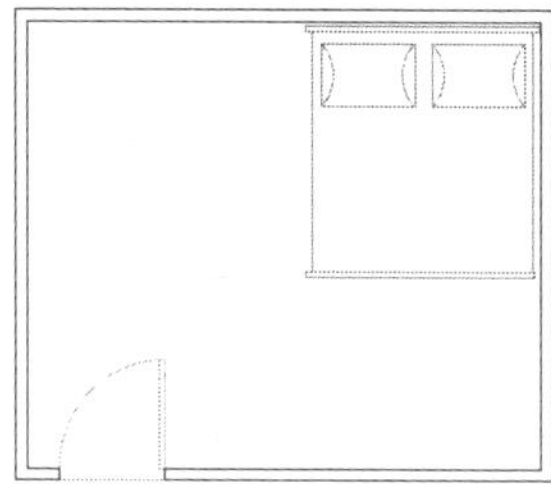

with the door.

- High-energy colours such as red should be avoided on walls and ceilings.
- Mirrors across from the bed or on the ceiling are not appropriate for a bedroom and can cause anxious restless feelings. Energy levels are lowest before going to sleep and upon waking and will be reflected back by the mirror.
- When encouraging or improving a relationship keep both sides of the bed open. Do not push one side against the wall.
- Keep the room free of clutter. Overstuffed closets and drawers create restlessness and fatigue. Clutter under beds can also affect sleep patterns.
- Bedrooms located over a garage are not auspicious. If this cannot be avoided be sure the garage is free of clutter, chemicals and in good repair.
- Pictures of action scenes or turbulent storms should

not be located across from your sleeping area.

- Place sachets of relaxing scents in pillowcases.
- **Ideal colours** for the bedroom are blue, green, beige and violet.
- Babies and young children's bedrooms are best next to the master bedroom, where teenagers rooms can be located at a distance.

HOME OFFICES OR WORK AREAS

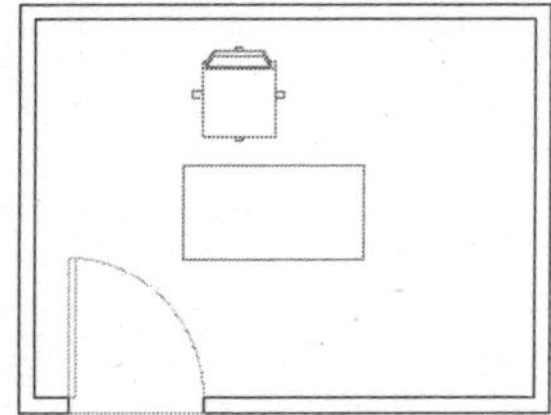

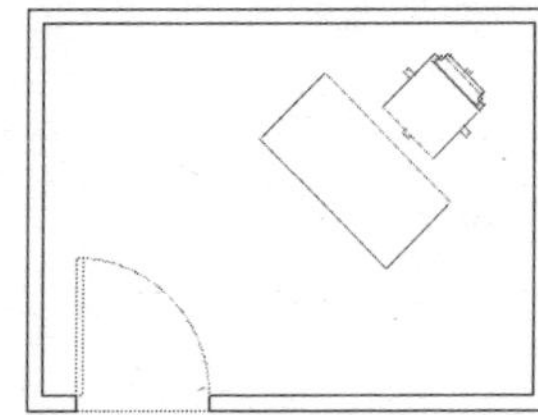

Position desks so that your back is to a solid wall and you have a clear view of the door

- Home based offices are best located close to the front or back door to keep customers from entering the main areas of your home.
- Desks and chairs should have their backs against a wall and be positioned in the power position of the room (farthest corner from the door).
- When backs are to the door positon a mirror on the screen or desk so that the door can be seen.
- Keep work areas free of clutter. Discard or remove

all excess paperwork that is not regularly used or needed. Store files in closed boxes or file cabinets and keep bills out of sight.

- Work areas should be well lit and inspiring. Be sure that the light is not causing shadows over the work area. Dull lights and shadows cause fatigue.
- Best colours for home offices are blue and green.

Sitting at a desk with your back to a door is bad Feng Shui.

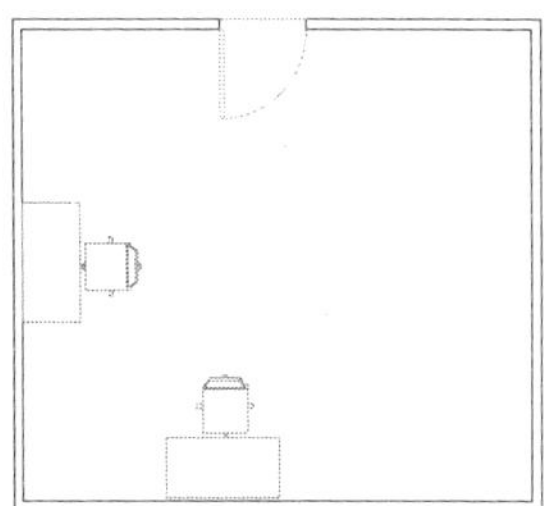

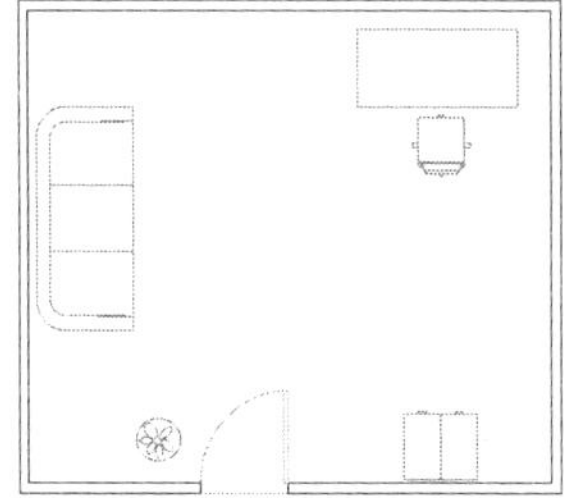

The two office layouts below are auspicous for the employees

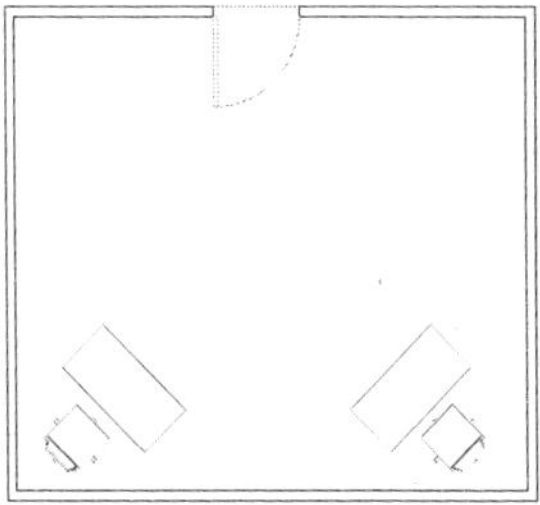

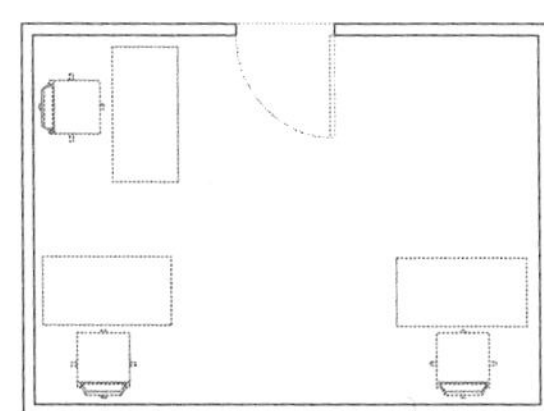

CLASSROOMS

☯ When setting up a classroom the teacher should-not be positioned so that their back is to the door as students will become distracted.

GENERAL TIPS

☯ Blank walls in a home say nothing. Walls are great for communicating messages of relaxation and inspiration. Hang decorative objects, pictures, photos and certificates in appropriate areas (see Pa Kua). Carefully select what you display in the children's room as they are easily influenced by the images they look at regularly.

☯ Use the Pa Kua as a guide to selecting colour and room position. Refer to your personal Kua directions to help select the best compass direction, solve problems and activate goals.

☯ Remove dried flowers and dead or decaying plants out of a room . They create stale energy and make you feel unmotivated, tired and lifeless. Fresh plants and cut flowers are best to uplift energy.

☯ When decorating keep in mind the purpose of the room, the creative cycles of the elements and yin and yang balance.

☯ All rooms should have all of the five elements represented by way of element, colour, object or shape.

The classroom layout below is not the most beneficial. Students may become distracted when facing the door

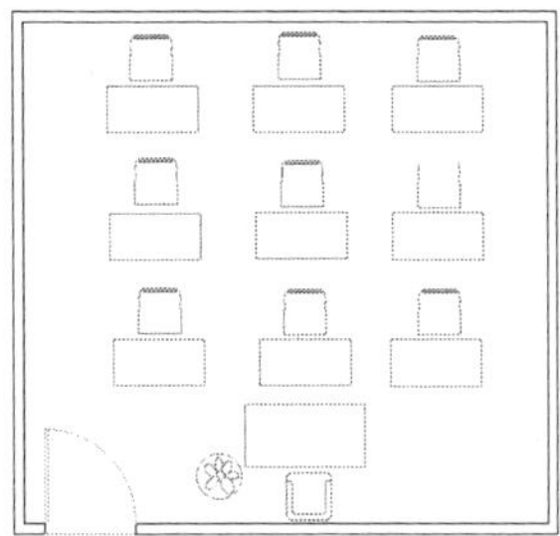

The classroom layouts below are auspicous for both teacher and student

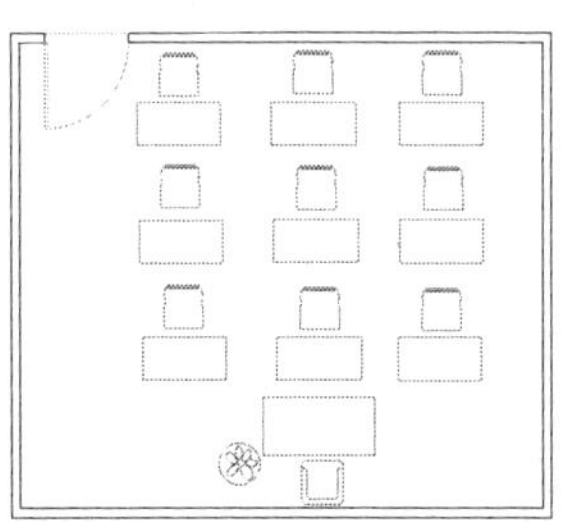

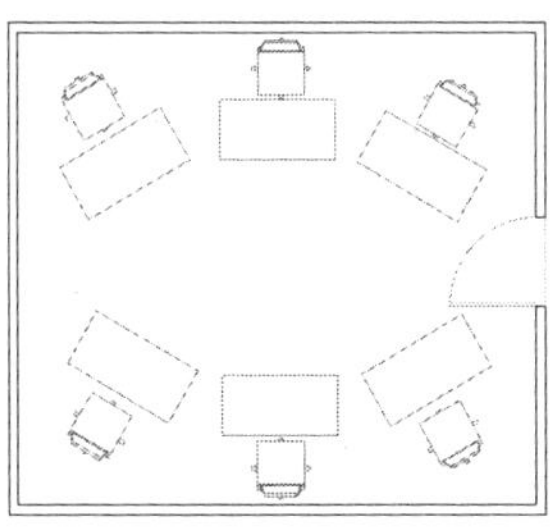

CHAPTER SIX

CASE STUDIES

FAMILY TIES

Melanie had not had contact with her natural father since childhood. After having a Feng Shui consultation she began to make changes to her home. One of the first areas she concentrated on was the study that faced East. She removed most of the clutter and gave it a fresh coat of paint. Finally she framed several photos of her and her father and hung them on the East wall of the Den. Three days later, she received a phone call from one of her Cousins, inviting her to a family reunion, at which her father was expected to attend. She was elated.

RELATIONSHIP IN TROUBLE

Robert and Sara moved into a two-bedroom basement apartment. After a few months they began to feel restless and fatigued. As a result, they were constantly arguing about trivial things. After hearing about Feng Shui, Sara arranged to have a consultant visit her home. The first thing that the consultant pointed out to the couple was the lighting in the apartment. The only natural light that came in was from the small living room window. The basement was high enough that the window let in some light, however the view was that of a brick wall. She suggested that they place several potted plants on the window ledge. Next she suggested that they change the bulbs to full-spectrum to bring in more of a natural light. In addition to the lighting the consultant suggested that they change the colour of the walls from dull beige to a soft yellow. She also stressed that they remove the brown shaggy carpet or replace it with a small area rug. The eager couple systematically made the required changes. Within a few weeks the couple noticed that their energy level had gone up and that they were not arguing as much. Sara was so excited about their newly Feng Shui'd apartment that she kept inviting friends over for dinner thereby improving their social life.

FINANCIAL STRESS

Ellen and Jeff were experiencing financial difficulties. Jeff was a self-employed contractor and experiencing financial stress. Ellen, a hairdresser was eight months pregnant and could not work as many hours as needed. They were falling behind in their mortgage payments and bills kept piling up. Finally they decided to call in a Feng Shui Practitioner to do a reading of their home. The first thing that their reading revealed was that the wealth area of their home was missing. The wealth area occupied a section of the yard that was littered with clutter and debris. On the advice of the consultant Jeff immediately cleared away the debris and replaced it with a birdbath and also added a few shrubs to the area. Exactly two days after clearing the area Jeff received a phone call from a client offering him a large contract. The condition of the contract was that he was to begin immediately and that he would be given a deposit upon signing the deal. The deposit alone was enough to get the couple back on track with their bills and even left enough that Ellen could stop working and relax during the last month of her pregnancy.

ATTRACTING LOVE

All of Carl's friends were either married or had steady girlfriends. At the age of 28 he felt ready to handle a serious relationship but was having no luck. His sister had given him a gift certificate for a Feng Shui consultation earlier that year for his birthday. After staring at it for months he finally got brave and set up an appointment to have his apartment Feng Shui'd. After chatting with Carl the consultant began to suggest a number of cures to help remedy his situation. She suggested that he remove some of the somewhat crude nude photographs from his living room wall and replace them with less graphic ones. Carl was a great photographer and enjoyed displaying his works of art. He was particularly fascinated with body piercing and tattoos of all types. After some discussion around the subject Carl immediately pulled out his portfolio with his collection of other prize-winning photos that he had taken. The consultant was shocked to see some of the most beautiful photos that she had ever laid eyes on. There were photos of birds in flight, swans, ducks and beautiful people including babies with their mothers. The consultant strongly suggested that Carl display some of these exquisite photos on his walls to replace the crude ones. The consultant gave Carl several other tips and remedies that he could apply including the idea of putting things in pairs rather then in one's. Feeling somewhat motivated Carl framed and displayed photos that the consultant suggested. He also purchased a small water fountain and put it by his front door. Soon after he made the changes he decided to invite a few friends over to check out the new look. One of his friend's wives brought along her sister Susan. Carl was very interested in this girl and she was fascinated by his artwork. As it worked out Susan was a wildlife artist and was thrilled to see this type of display. Carl's social life literally improved overnight and is now engaged to be married to Susan.

INCREASING RETAIL SALES

Fenella followed the recommendation of a friend and had a Feng Shui professional do a reading of her Lingerie store, two weeks after opening. The reading revealed that the window was monochromatic and did not clearly reflect the merchandise. Because Fenella had not yet purchased all her display figures she was able to purchase navy blue and also white (partial) mannequins to display the lingerie in the window. These colours were most auspicious for the Northeast facing window. It was suggested that the addition of spot lighting would be beneficial to attract attention of passing traffic at night. A crystal was recommended to for the window to attract positive energy and dispel the split energy caused by the tree out front. An attractive wooden sign that hung from a metal bracket, painted with gold stars on a white background was recommended to reflect the logo and be in harmony with the most auspicious elements for that direction. The suspended sign would attract attention of pedestrians and traffic alike. Following these few recommendations Fenella experienced a substantial increase in customer traffic and sales.

CAREER CHANGE

Since moving into their new home Jim and Diane were constantly arguing about everything. One week after moving in Diane lost her job of 10 years. A friend suggested that they attend a Feng Shui Workshop to see if perhaps this was something that could help them put their life back in order. They had heard stories of how a home's energy can effect it's occupants so they both were open to the idea of Feng Shui. While at the workshop they realized that the direction of the front door was not in good harmony with their own personal best directions. Another problem was that their front door which faced north had been painted red, which created further conflict. However they faced their biggest challenge when they realized that they had a road directly pointed to their front door. After the workshop that evening, they decided that they would call in a Feng Shui expert to help remedy the disharmony in their home. After a short interview the consultant suggested that they first thing they do is repaint the door a navy blue colour and add a shiny gold door knocker in the middle. Next she suggested that they hang a hollow wind chime on the front porch and hang up a flowering planter on the other side. She also suggested that they replace the low wattage front bulb with a stronger one. In the inside of the front entrance she suggested placing a small water fountain and a door mat, preferably red and brown.

After listening to all the reccommendations the couple decided to begin with the front entrance. Within a week they had changed the colour of the door, added a brown mat, hung a windchime outside and added a flowering planter. They were so busy making these changes that they didn't even notice that they were not arguing. Finally, they went shopping for a water fountain. Just as they were paying for it Diane received a call on her cell phone. Several weeks ago she had inquired, through a friend about the possiblity of working at her bank. At the time there was nothing available. The call was from the same bank offering her a key position with a handsome salary. Naturally she was pleased and excited. They took their fountain home placed in near the front door and decided that they would continue to Feng Shui their home a little at a time.

CHAPTER SEVEN

SEVEN STEP FENG SHUI

Now you can Feng Shui your own home or office space simply by following this step by step process. As you go through these steps refer back to sections of the book that are being referred to. There are plenty of charts and references that will help guide you to the right choices. In many cases you will come up with ideas of your own that will work just as well as those suggested in this book. Don't worry if it takes you a while to finally click into the flow of things as this is normal. Feng Shui is not something you can learn in a day, month or year. It takes most masters a lifetime of study to really understand all the principles of Feng Shui. With these seven steps you can now begin the process of putting your life back into balance a step at a time.

1. EDUCATE YOURSELF

The first step is to educate yourself on Feng Shui, the art of placement. Now that you have read this far, you have begun the process of understanding. Feng Shui is a very complex system and because there are so many views on the subject it can seem confusing to the beginner.

· Read many books on Feng Shui. Check the the recommended reading section for suggestions.

· Make an effort to attend regular workshops and seminars on the subject.

· Subscribe to magazines and newsletters to keep yourself updated.

Test your knowledge

1. Feng Shui is an ancient art that began in China around 618 AD. Give examples of how it can help in today's modern world?

2. Name the Five Energies, their associated colours, shape and characteristics.

3. What element colour commands attention? What element colour helps promote relaxation.?

5. If there were too much of the fire element in a room what element would you add to reduce its effect?

6. How can compass direction help create a balanced space?

7. What colours and shapes would you find dominating a yin space?

2. CLARIFY YOUR GOALS

Identify your goals and concerns by answering these questions.

On a scale of 0-6 rate areas of your life.

0 - non existent   1 - bad   2 - not good

3 - average   4 - not bad   5 - good

6 - excellent

For your residence answer question a) and for work spaces refer to b)

MENTORS/HELPFUL PEOPLE

1.a) I always have the help of others when I need it.
   b) same as above

KNOWLEDGE

2. a) I make an effort to learn something new every day.
   b) same as above

CAREER

3. a) I am happy with my present career choice.
   b) My job is satisfying, rewarding and fulfilling

CHILDREN/CREATIVITY

4. a) I am happy with my children's development and/or I am expressing my creativity to it's fullest
   b) I am expressing my creativity and developing new projects and ideas.

PERSONAL RELATIONSHIP

5. a) My love life is happy and fulfilling.
   b) I have a good relationship with my partner/ customers.

FAMILY

6. a) I have a good relationship with my family, friends and community.
   b) I get along with my co-workers, business associates and work community.

WEALTH

7. a) I am comfortable with my financial situation and feel self empowered.
   b) same as above

LIFE ASPIRATIONS CHART
Easy Reference Chart

SECTION	COLOUR	SHAPES	OBJECTS	DIRECTION
KNOWLEDGE Wisdom	Blue, Green, Earthtones	Curved, Rectangle	Books, Magazines, Pictures of Mountains	Northeast
CAREER Self	Blue,Green, White	Curved	Office Equipment Charts, Aquarium	North
MENTORS Helpful People	Blue, White,Violet	Curved,Round	Pictures or Statues of Angels, Saints, teach-ers or Guides	Northwest
CHILDREN Creativity	White, Blue Earthtones	Round	Pictures of children, Crafts & Artwork, Piano, Windchimes	West
RELATIONSHIP Marriage	Red,Earthtones	Traingle,Square	Paired objects, can-dles, Plants & flowers	Southwest
FUTURE Fame	Red,Green, Earthtones	Triangle	Trophies, certificates, Crystals, Lights, Plants	South
WEALTH Power	Green,Red	Rectangle	Crystals, Flowers, fountains, fish bowl, Items of value	Southeast
FAMILY Community	Green, Blue, Red	Rectangle	Family & Ancestors group pictures, plants, fountain	East

FUTURE/REPUTATION

8. a) I have clearly defined my future goals.
   b) I have a good reputation in my business and am achieving my goals.

Pay particular attention to the questions that you rated from (0-3). Make a list of these areas of concern. Refer to the Pa Kua grid in chapter three. Overlay the grid on your floor plan by lining up compass direction of the Pa Kua to the compass direction of your home. The eight pie shaped sections of the Pa Kua relate to the eight life aspirations. Work only on the areas of your life that need to be fixed. For example if you rated your career as a 2 then refer to the north sector of the Pa Kua.

3. REMOVE CLUTTER, CLEAR BLOCKS AND PROPER MAINTENANCE

CLUTTER

Begin by removing the clutter from areas of concern. Clutter stagnates the flow of energy in a space. Every item, object and thought is attached to us by a tiny thread and pulls and tugs at our every thought. A good rule to remember is that if you don't need it, like it or want it, get rid of it. Look inside your closets, cupboards, under beds and behind doors, under the stairs, in the garage and in the back yard. If you are deeply attached to some of your items and have difficulty discarding them, store them in plastic, see through tubs and put them away in a storage area.

BLOCKS

Blocks are items or objects that stop the flow of energy. These items and objects are particularly inauspicious on pathways, entrances, windows, hallways and foyers. For example, if you are faced with the side view of a large wall unit upon entering a front entrance the area becomes stale and blocked creating an un welcoming feeling. When the view from a window is a brick wall or large obstruction it creates an oppressed feeling . When the block cannot be removed, create a diversion or soften the effect by using plants, screens or a window dressing treatment.

MAINTENANCE

The outside of your home or office reflects how you feel about yourself. First impressions are usually lasting impressions so keep the outside of your building well maintained. Remove weeds, dead plants and fallen branches, fill in holes, cracks, and discard or fix all damaged objects and items. Replace old roof tiles and remove peeling paint from windowsills and walls. Replace all burnt out bulbs. Be sure that the front entrance has a bright bulb. Most important of all be sure your front door opens and closes properly.

Maintaining the inside of a building is equally important as the outside. When the inside walls, windows, doors and ceilings and plumbing are cracked, rusted or falling apart it creates feelings of stagnation and staleness, resulting in a lack of energy for those living around it. Burnt out bulbs, broken furniture and appliances that aren't working create unrest and an anxious feeling making the occupant feel frustrated, tired and lifeless. Keeping the inside of your space in good repair and in working order allows the chi energy to flow freely.

4. POSITIONING THE GRID AND YOUR PERSONAL KUA

Use the Pa Kua to locate which area of your home relates to areas of your life. When possible rooms can be selected according to the grid. For example a perfect location for your office would be in the career or wealth area of your home. Be aware that all of these areas are connected to a compass direction, elements and colours. To keep balance and harmony select colours items and objects and patterns that best reflect the area of the Pa Kua. The grid can be a valuable tool in helping restore balance in your life.

Refer to the cycles of the five elements to help put balance back into a space that is out of balance. An example of this would be when a room has too much blue(water) use the reducing cycle of the elements and add wood (green) to reduce the energy of the water. If there is too much fire energy in a room use earth (brown) to reduce its affect or you can use the domination cycle and bring in the element of water (blue or black) to overpower the fire energy. The cycle of creation is used to keep things in balance. If you want to add colours and design a space use the creative cycle of the elements to keep things in harmony. If you would like to decorate a room in earth tones use fire and metal to complement the tones. Fire creates earth and earth creates metal. All of these elements are connected and work well together.

WOOD → FIRE → EARTH → METAL → WATER →

Use the charts to identify your own personal Kua number and find which are your personal best directions (chapter 4) . Once you set your goals position yourself in your best directions and avoid sitting or sleeping in your inauspicious directions. Use the guidelines and tips in this book to avoid positioning yourself in line with negative energies such as poison arrows or under beams or directly lined up with the door.

Once you know your Kua number you can determine if you are in harmony with your front door, refer to charts 90-91 in the appendix.

5. POSITIONING OF FURNITURE AND OBJECTS AND SELF

Furniture should be positioned in a manner that allows the chi to flow freely around all sides. If you have too much furniture, relocate what you don't use, like or need.

Make sure that the furniture is not pushed up against the wall or arranged too closely together. Whenever possible sofas and chairs should be positioned backing on to a wall, not with the back to an entrance or window. Cover up any poison arrows or sharp edges, protruding corners by covering them up or softening them with plants. (see cures section)
Check the colours, pattern and shape of the furniture and balance the elements to create harmony in the room . For example, if the sofa were low square, brown and heavy it would be an earth element. Earth is very yin energy and makes you feel grounded. If this

were not your goal for the room then you would need to balance and uplift the energy of the room by adding fire shapes and colours. Position objects pictures and other items according to their significance. For example certificates are best in the career or future locations and if you want to attract a love interest put things in pairs and in your relationship area.

Position yourself in the power area of a room when self empowerment is needed. The power area is the farthest corner away from the door. By positioning yourself in this area you have the most advantage over the room. In the case where there are two doors consider the one that is most used and keep the other door closed or blocked.

6. APPLYING CURES AND ACTIVATING SECTORS

Once all of the clutter and blocks have been removed from an area it is time to apply remedies and cures and activate.. Cure problematic areas by using suggestions outlined in the cure section of the book. Then begin to activate areas of concern by adding special objects, or items that have meaning and bring energy to the space in question.

To cure and activate a missing area of a room or space use the following method. If the area is missing from a room and has a protruding wall that faces into the space, remedy it by putting a plant or softening the affect of the edge. In the case where the missing area rests in the back or front yard use lights, shrubs, plants or decorative stones to finish or square off the area. Be sure the area is free of clutter and well maintained. If the missing area is one of the areas that you rated low be sure to activate it by adding some bright lights, water or something to add life to it such as a bird bath or bird feeder.

Refer to the cure chapter and the appendix section as guides to help select cures. Time should be taken to carefully select the cures and remedies that you feel comfortable with. Use your intuition to guide you and if something does not feel right then don't use it. Colours, smell, light, sound and touch can also be used alone or in combination with the other cures.

7. GOING WITH THE FLOW

The final step in Feng Shui is the simplest of all. Your attitude and intention can make the difference between failure and success. If you think it won't work then you are probably right. If your intentions are to hurt someone else to benefit yourself, you will surely fail. Positive attitude and pure intention will bring you favourable results.

While going through all of the steps think of how balance and harmony can enhance your life and the life of others. Feng Shui is not a magic genie that can be summoned every time you need help, it is rather a way of living your life in harmony simply by using the rhythms of nature.

Finally, apply the Taoist theory of Wu Wei, the law of "non doing". Make all of the necessary changes then let go. Things will happen naturally and in their own time. If you are too anxious and try to force things to happen you will be going against the grain. Simply sit back, relax and go with the flow. ☯

APPENDICES

CHARTS

CHINESE LUNAR CALENDAR

Year	Begins
1924	Feb 5
1925	Jan 24
1926	Feb 13
1927	Feb 2
1928	Jan 23
1929	Feb 10
1930	Jan 30
1931	Feb 17
1932	Feb 6
1933	Jan 26
1934	Feb 14
1935	Feb 4
1936	Jan 24
1937	Feb 11
1938	Jan 31
1939	Feb 19
1940	Feb 8
1941	Jan 27
1942	Feb 15
1943	Feb 5
1944	Jan 25
1945	Feb 13
1946	Feb 2
1947	Jan 22
1948	Feb 10
1949	Jan 29
1950	Feb 17
1951	Feb 6
1952	Jan 27
1953	Feb 14
1954	Feb 3
1955	Jan 24
1956	Feb 12
1957	Jan 31
1958	Feb 18
1959	Feb 8
1960	Jan 28
1961	Feb 15
1962	Feb 5
1963	Jan 25
1964	Feb 13

Year	Begins
1965	Feb 2
1966	Jan 21
1967	Feb 9
1968	Jan 30
1969	Feb 17
1970	Feb 6
1971	Jan 27
1972	Feb 15
1973	Feb 3
1974	Jan 23
1975	Feb 11
1976	Jan 31
1977	Feb 18
1978	Feb 7
1979	Jan 28
1980	Feb 16
1981	Feb 5
1982	Jan 25
1983	Feb 13
1984	Feb 2
1985	Feb 20
1986	Feb 9
1987	Jan 29
1988	Feb 17
1989	Feb 6
1990	Jan 27
1991	Feb 15
1992	Feb 4
1993	Jan 23
1994	Feb 10
1995	Jan 31
1996	Feb 19
1997	Feb 8
1998	Jan 28
1999	Feb 6
2000	Feb 5
2001	Jan 24
2002	Feb 12
2003	Feb 1

PERSONAL KUA NUMBERS

Birth Year	Male	Female
1924	4	2
1925	3	3
1926	2	4
1927	1	8
1928	9	6
1929	8	7
1930	7	8
1931	6	9
1932	2	1
1933	4	2
1934	3	3
1935	2	4
1936	1	8
1937	9	6
1938	8	7
1939	7	8
1940	6	9
1941	2	1
1942	4	2
1943	3	3
1944	2	4
1945	1	8
1946	9	6
1947	8	7
1948	7	8
1949	6	9
1950	2	1
1951	4	2
1952	3	3
1953	2	4
1954	1	8
1955	9	6
1956	8	7
1957	7	8
1958	6	9
1959	2	1
1960	4	2
1961	3	3
1962	2	4
1963	1	8
1964	9	6
1965	8	7
1966	7	8
1967	6	9
1968	2	1
1969	4	2
1970	3	3
1971	2	4
1972	1	8
1973	9	6
1974	8	7
1975	7	8
1976	6	9
1977	2	1
1978	4	2
1979	3	3
1980	2	4
1981	1	8
1982	9	6
1983	8	7
1984	7	8
1985	6	9
1986	2	1
1987	4	2
1988	3	3
1989	2	4
1990	1	8
1991	9	6
1992	8	7
1993	7	8
1994	6	9
1995	2	1
1996	4	2
1997	3	3
1998	2	4
1999	1	8
2000	9	6
2001	8	7
2002	7	8
2003	6	9
2004	2	1
2005	4	2
2006	3	3
2007	2	4

KUA NUMBER DESCRIPTION

KUA NUMBER	COLOURS	SHAPES	DIRECTION	SECONDARY DIRECTIONS
1 - Water	Black, Navy	Curved	North	West, Northwest, East Southeast
2 - Earth	Brown, Beige	Square	Southwest	West, Northwest, Northeast, South
3 - Wood	Green	Rectangle	East	North, Southeast, South
4 - Wood	Green	Rectangle	Southeast	North, East, South
5 - Earth	Brown, Beige	Square	Centre	Southwest,West,Northwest,Northeast,South
6 - Metal	White	Round	Northwest	Southwest,West,North,Northeast
7 - Metal	White	Round	West	Southwest,Northwest,North,Northeast
8 - Earth	Brown, Beige	Square	Northeast	Southwest,West,Northwest,South
9 - Fire	Red	Triangle	South	East,Southeast, Southwest, Northeast

KUA NUMBER DOOR DIRECTION

DIRECTION OF FRONT DOOR COLOUR	KUA NUM	HARMONY (H) CONFLICT (C)	TO REMEDY ADD
NORTH	1	H	-
	2	C	WHITE
	3	H	-
	4	H	-
	6	H	-
	7	H	-
	8	C	WHITE
	9	C	BLUE, GREEN
SOUTH	1	C	GREEN, BLUE
	2	H	-
	3	H	-
	4	H	-
	6	C	EARTHTONES
	7	C	EARTHTONES
	8	H	-
	9	H	-
EAST	1	H	-
	2	C	RED
	3	H	-
	4	H	-
	6	C	BLUE, BLACK
	7	C	BLUE, BLACK
	8	C	RED
	9	H	-
WEST	1	H	-
	2	H	-
	3	C	BLUE, BLACK
	4	C	BLUE, BLACK
	6	H	-
	7	H	-
	8	H	-
	9	H	-

KUA NUMBER DOOR DIRECTION - Continued

DIRECTION OF FRONT DOOR COLOUR	KUA NUM	HARMONY (H) CONFLICT (C)	TO REMEDY ADD
NORTHEAST	1	C	WHITE
	2	H	-
	3	C	RED
	4	C	RED
	6	H	-
	7	H	-
	8	H	-
	9	H	-
NORTHWEST	1	H	-
	2	H	-
	3	C	BLUE, BLACK
	4	C	BLUE, BLACK
	6	H	-
	7	H	-
	8	H	-
	9	C	BROWN
SOUTHEAST	1	H	-
	2	C	RED
	3	H	-
	4	H	-
	6	C	BLUE, BLACK
	7	C	BLUE, BLACK
	8	C	RED
	9	H	-
SOUTHWEST	1	C	WHITE
	2	H	-
	3	C	RED
	4	C	RED
	6	H	-
	7	H	-
	8	H	-
	9	H	-

CHINESE ZODIAC SIGN AND YEAR ELEMENT

**note the year element is the ruling element*

Birth Year	Animal Sign	Ruling Element	Birth Year	Animal Sign	Ruling Element
1900	Rat	Metal	1954	Horse	Wood
1901	Ox	Metal	1955	Goat	Wood
1902	Tiger	Water	1956	Monkey	Fire
1903	Rabbit	Water	1957	Rooster	Fire
1904	Dragon	Wood	1958	Dog	Earth
1905	Snake	Wood	1959	Pig	Earth
1906	Horse	Fire	1960	Rat	Metal
1907	Goat	Fire	1961	Ox	Metal
1908	Monkey	Earth	1962	Tiger	Water
1909	Rooster	Earth	1963	Rabbit	Water
1910	Dog	Metal	1964	Dragon	Wood
1911	Pig	Metal	1965	Snake	Wood
1912	Rat	Water	1966	Horse	Fire
1913	Ox	Water	1967	Goat	Fire
1914	Tiger	Wood	1968	Monkey	Earth
1915	Rabbit	Wood	1969	Rooster	Earth
1916	Dragon	Fire	1970	Dog	Metal
1917	Snake	Fire	1971	Pig	Metal
1918	Horse	Earth	1972	Rat	Water
1919	Ram	Earth	1973	Ox	Water
1920	Monkey	Metal	1974	Tiger	Wood
1921	Rooster	Metal	1975	Rabbit	Wood
1922	Dog	Water	1976	Dragon	Fire
1923	Pig	Water	1977	Snake	Fire
1924	Rat	Wood	1978	Horse	Earth
1925	Ox	Wood	1979	Goat	Earth
1926	Tiger	Fire	1980	Monkey	Metal
1927	Rabbit	Fire	1981	Rooster	Metal
1928	Dragon	Earth	1982	Dog	Water
1929	Snake	Earth	1983	Pig	Water
1930	Horse	Metal	1984	Rat	Wood
1931	Goat	Metal	1985	Ox	Wood
1932	Monkey	Water	1986	Tiger	Fire
1933	Rooster	Water	1987	Rabbit	Fire
1934	Dog	Wood	1988	Dragon	Earth
1935	Pig	Wood	1989	Snake	Earth
1936	Rat	Fire	1990	Horse	Metal
1937	Ox	Fire	1991	Goat	Metal
1938	Tiger	Earth	1992	Monkey	Water
1939	Rabbit	Earth	1993	Rooster	Water
1940	Dragon	Metal	1994	Dog	Wood
1941	Snake	Metal	1995	Pig	Wood
1942	Horse	Water	1996	Rat	Fire
1943	Goat	Water	1997	Ox	Fire
1944	Monkey	Wood	1998	Tiger	Earth
1945	Rooster	Wood	1999	Rabbit	Earth
1946	Dog	Fire	2000	Dragon	Metal
1947	Pig	Fire	2001	Snake	Metal
1948	Rat	Earth	2002	Horse	Water
1949	Ox	Earth	2003	Goat	Water
1950	Tiger	Metal	2004	Monkey	Wood
1951	Rabbit	Metal	2005	Rooster	Wood
1952	Dragon	Water	2006	Dog	Fire
1953	Snake	Water	2007	Pig	Fire

CHINESE ZODIAC SIGN DESCRIPTION

*note: the **dominant element** refers to that of the animals personality which is different from the **ruling element***

Rat Intelligent, imaginative, opportunistic, elegant, affectionate, alert, practical, quickly learns from experience, charming, placid, passionate, sentimental, constructive critic, honest and materialistic. Dominant element is Water and the best colour is black.

Ox Conscientious, hard-working, serious, strong, persistent, clear-thinking, practical, patient, reliable, gentle, careful, determined and capable. Dominant element is Water and the best colours are black, green and dark green.

Tiger Honourable, protective, ambitious, daring, idealistic, determined, benevolent, loyal, wise, generous, charismatic, fortunate, courageous and sensitive. Dominant element is Wood and the best colours are black, green and dark green.

Rabbit Circumspect, sensitive, discreet, reflective, principles, hospitable, expressive, diplomatic, peaceful, intuitive, moderate, well organized, refined, intelligent and honourable. Dominant element is Wood and the best colours are green and blue.

Dragon Intelligent, exciting, irresistible, voluble, healthy, sentimental, enthusiastic, successful, lucky, scrupulous, perfectionist, idealistic, dynamic and visionary. Dominant element is Wood and the best colours are blue, green, pink, red and purple.

Snake Organized, reflective, curious, sensual, gregarious, wise, sophisticated, lucid, perceptive, profound, shrewd, self-contained, elegant and distinguished. Dominant element is Fire and the best colours are blue, green, pink, red and purple.

Horse Loyal, noble, cheerful, enthusiastic, enterprising, flexible, sincere, frank, versatile, talkative, gregarious, generous, unselfish, realist and energetic. Dominant element is Fire and the best colours are red and pink.

Goat Creative, imaginative, ingenious, honest, capricious, sensitive, faithful, sincere, peaceful, adaptable, independent, ardent, elegant, gentle and easy-going. Dominant element is Fire and the best colours are brown, red and pink.

EASTERN ZODIAC SIGNS - continued

Monkey Independent, sociable, enthusiastic, lively, sensitive, optimistic, audacious, inventive, astute, vivacious, tolerant, quick-witted, generous, entertaining and gregarious. Dominant element is Metal and the best colours are brown, red and pink.

Rooster Honest, courageous, resilient, relaxed, loyal, capable, charitable, obliging, flamboyant, enthusiastic, cultivated, sincere, generous and entertaining. Dominant element is Metal and the dominant colour is white.

Dog Sensitive, witty, courageous, imaginative, unselfish, moralistic, understanding, tolerant, trustworthy, responsible, honest, noble, faithful, dutiful, idealistic and loyal. Dominant element is Metal and the best colours are white, grey and black.

Pig Cheerful, honest, generous, uncomplaining, sensual, tolerant,, optimistic, diligent, peaceful, determined, courteous, careful, fortunate and eager. Dominant element is Water and the best colours are white, grey and black.

OPPOSITES

The Rat and the Horse.
The Ox and the Goat.
The Tiger and the Monkey.
The Rabbit and the Rooster.
The Dragon and the Dog.
The Snake and the Pig.

COMPATIBLE PARTNERS

The Rat, the Dragon and the Monkey.
The Ox, the Snake and the Rooster.
The Tiger, the Horse and the Dog.
The Rabbit, the Goat and the Pig.

WESTERN ASTROLOGY

ARIES	March 21 to April 19
Symbol	Ram
Planet	Mars
Colour	Scarlet
Stone	Diamond
Element	Fire
Flower	Red rose and gladioli
Match	Aries, Leo and Sagittarius
Opposites	Cancer and Pisces

TAURUS	April 20 to May 20
Symbol	Bull
Planet	Venus
Colour	Green, Blue and Cream
Stone	Emerald and Jade
Element	Earth
Flower	Carnation and Rose
Match	Virgo and Capricorn
Opposites	Gemini and Aquarius

GEMINI	May 21 to June 20
Symbol	Twins
Planet	Mercury
Colour	White and Light Yellow
Stone	Agate
Element	Air
Flower	Chyrsanthemum
Match	Gemini, Libra and Aquarius
Opposites	Taurus, Cancer, Scorpio and Capricorn

CANCER	June 21 to July 22
Symbol	Crab
Planet	Moon
Colour	Silver and Green
Stone	Moonstone
Element	Water
Flower	Lily
Match	Scoprio and Pisces
Opposites	Aries, Gemini and Aquarius

WESTERN ASTROLOGY - continued

LEO	July 23 to August 22
Symbol	Lion
Planet	Sun
Colour	Gold, flame orange and bright yellow
Stone	Ruby
Element	Fire
Flower	Poppy
Match	Aries, Leo and Sagittarius
Opposites	Virgo and Libra

VIRGO	August 23 to September 22
Symbol	Virgin/Maiden
Planet	Mercury
Colour	Dark Green, Blue and Brown
Stone	Sapphire
Element	Earth
Flower	Anemone
Match	Taurus, Virgo and Capricorn
Opposites	Leo, Libra and Sagittarius

LIBRA	September 23 to October 22
Symbol	Scales
Planet	Venus
Colour	Lavender
Stone	Opal
Element	Air
Flower	Rose
Match	Gemini and Aquarius
Opposites	Leo, Virgo and Capricorn

SCORPIO	October 23 to November 21
Symbol	Scorpion
Planet	Pluto
Colour	Claret and Magenta
Stone	Topaz and Jasper
Element	Water
Flower	Chrysanthemum
Match	Cancer and Pisces
Opposites	Gemini, Sagittarius and Aquarius

WESTERN ASTROLOGY - continued

SAGITTARIUS	November 22 to December 21
Symbol	Archer
Planet	Jupiter
Colour	Turquoise and Indigo
Stone	Turquoise
Element	Fire
Flower	Narcissus
Match	Aries, Leo and Sagittarius
Opposites	Virgo, Scorpio, Capricorn and Pisces

CAPRICORN	December 22 to January 19
Symbol	Goat
Planet	Saturn
Colour	Blue
Stone	Garnet and Onyx
Element	Earth
Flower	Carnation
Match	Taurus, Virgo and Capricorn
Opposites	Gemini, Libra, Sagittarius and Aquarius

AQUARIUS	January 20 to February 18
Symbol	Water Bearer
Planet	Uranus
Colour	Azure Blue
Stone	Amethyst
Element	Air
Flower	Violet
Match	Gemini, Libra and Aquarius
Opposites	Taurus, Cancer, Scorpio and Capricorn

PISCES	February 19 to March 20
Symbol	Fish
Planet	Neptune
Colour	Sea Green
Stone	Aquamarine and Bloodstone
Element	Water
Flower	Lilac
Match	Cancer, Scorpio and Pisces
Opposites	Aries and Sagittarius

COLOURS

Red	Happiness, prosperity, inspirational, exciting, dynamic, powerful and energetic
Yellow	Positiveness, optimism, cheerful, elevating, stimulating and brightening
Green	Peace, tranquility, harmony, soothing, restful, relaxing, growth, immaturity, nurturing and rejuvenating
Blue	Optimism, security, thoughtfulness, constancy, truth, calming, introspective, responsible, tran quil, spirituality, intuition, isolation, adventure, independent, investigative, mysterious and unique
Violet	Spirituality, high ideals, wonder, restful, creativity, idealism, mysticism and inspiration
Gold	Dignity, money, honour, fame, positive, opti mistic, dignified, good luck and wealth
White	Purity, brightness, innocence, untainted, godli ness, cleanliness and freshness
Black	Intensity, formality, sophistication, gloomy, dynamic, money, mystery, independence, intrigue, strength and solidarity

NUMBERS

1. Honour and luck

2. Double luck, double happiness, good number

3. Unbalanced, unstable, can mean growth

4. Change, death, should be combined with a lucky number

5. Denotes balance, transformation and fullness

6. Denotes the six emotions, sexual union, spiritual dimensions

7. Seven planets, seven days of the week, seven ages, lucky number

8. Power, wealth and great wisdom

9. Strength, long life and perception

SCENTS

Lavender	Relaxation, calm, serene, peaceful, tranquility, comfort, soothing, restful, protection and healing.
Jasmine	Sensual, harmony, exotic, optimism, well-being, soothing, balancing, euphoric, comforting, inspirational, confidence, good luck in love and wealth, aphrodisiac, alleviates depression and tension and raises self esteem.
Chamomile	Soothing, sedative, relaxing, balancing, dissolves negativity, calming and stress-relieving.
Eucalyptus	Stimulating, clearing, refreshing, cooling, purifying, disinfecting, energizing and uplifting.
Lemon	Cleanliness, freshness, stimulating, purifying, refreshing, energetic, motivating, positive, uplifting and clearing.
Orange	Warming, uplifting, refreshing, energizing, cleansing, rejuvenating, joyful, purification, healing, abundance and happiness.
Patchouli	Aphrodisiac, relaxing, balancing, uplifting, stimulating, purifies and prosperity.
Peppermint	Cooling, refreshing, stimulating, purifies, attracts positive energies, revitalizes and rejuvenates.
Rosemary	Refreshing, stimulating, alleviates mental and physical fatigue, clearing, peaceful, contentment, attracts love, healing and rejuvenates.
Ylang Ylang	Aphrodisiac, calming, peaceful and relaxing

GLOSSARY

Auspicious
Favourable, fortunate, lucky, opportune

Celestial Animals
Four animal names, tortoise, dragon, phoenix and tiger, used to describe land formations.

Chi
Vital life force or energy that exists in everything in the cosmos. That which propels all in motion.

Compass School
The Feng Shui school that uses compass to determine the flow of chi at any given time in any given location.

Confucius
The name of a Chinese philosopher who studied the I Ching his entire life.

Elements
The Elements Wood, Fire, Earth, Metal and Water, according to the Chinese provide valuable information for the practice of Feng Shui.

Feng
Chinese character that means wind.

Five Elements
Water, wood, fire earth and metal.

Flying Star
A Feng Shui approach that uses star numbers that fly or move around the lo shu grid.

Shui
Chinese character that means water.

Feng Shui
Translated it means Wind Water, The Chinese Art of Placement. Harnessing the earth's natural energy and rhythms to achieve balance and harmony in a living space.

Form School
The Feng Shui school that analyzes location and land formations to determine the flow of chi.

GLOSSARY - continued

Geomancy
Divination or knowledge that measures the flow of energies above and below ground.

I Ching
An ancient Chinese philosophical text referred to as "The Book of Changes" , containing 64 hexigrams used for divination.

Inauspicious
Unfavourable, unfortunate, unlucky, inopportune.

Kua
A number that refers to one of the eight sides of the Pa Kua. A person's Kua number can determine their best compass direction and is calculated based on their year of birth.

Lo Shu
A magic square containing 9 numbers that adds up to 15 in any direction. When placed over the Pa Kua its numbers refer to various directions and aspirations.

Luo Pan
A Chinese Feng Shui compass used to determine good chi directions and times.

Pa Kua
Also referred to as Ba Gua, is an eight-sided trigram used to identify the implied meaning of space within an environment.

Poison Arrow
Also referred to as "secret arrow, sha chi" and "shars". A sharp edge or obstruction with sharp chi is directed towards a home or its occupant. The inauspicious fast moving chi creates negative energy.

Sha
Stagnant chi.

Tao
"The Way" or way of living life based on Taoist philosophy.

Taoism
The philosophical system based on an ancient text.

GLOSSARY - continued

Trigram
Three lines that are either broken or solid. When grouped in threes symbolize the combining of heaven, earth and man.

Yang
Active energy, one of two complimentary opposites and is the opposite of yin.

Yin
Passive energy, one of two complimentary opposites and is the opposite of yang.

BIBLIOGRAPHY

Collins Gem, Chinese Astrology, HARPER GEMS PUB. LONDON, 1996
ISBN 0-00-472296-5

Day, Laura, Practical Intuition-How to Harness the Power of Your Instinct and Make it Work for You, VILLARD, NEW YORK, 1996.
ISBN 0-679-44932-9

Gallagher, Winifred, The Power of Place-How Our Surroundings Shape Our Thoughts, Emotions, and Actions, FIRST HARPER PERENNIAL, NEW YORK, 1994.
ISBN 0-06-097602-0

Linn, Denise, Sacred Space, BALLANTINE BOOKS, NEW YORK, 1995.
ISBN 0-345-39769-X

Page, Michael, The Power of Chi, EQUARIAN PRESS, SAN FRAN.1988
ISBN 1-85538-363-2

Pearson, David, The New Natural House Book - FIRESIDE, NY., 1998.
ISBN 0-684-84733-7

Rossbach, Sarah and Yun, Lin, Living Color - Master Lin Yun's Guide to Feng Shui and the Art of Color, KODANSHA AMERICA, NEW YORK, 1994.
ISBN 1-56836-014-2

Simons, T. Raphael, Feng Shui Step by Step, CROWN PUB., NY. 1996
ISBN 0-517-88794-0

Too, Lillian, The Complete Illustrated Guide To Feng Shui, ELEMENT BOOKS, SHAFTSBURY, 1996.
ISBN 1-85230-902-4

Moran, Elizabeth, Biktashev, Val, TCIG on Feng Shui, ALPHA BOOKS, MCMILLAN PUBLISHING, NEW YORK 1999
ISBN 0-02-863106-6

Visconti, Lina, Seven Step Feng Shui, TM PUBLICATIONS, RICHMOND HILL, 1998.
ISBN 0-9684391-0-1

Wong, Eva, Feng-Shui- The Ancient Wisdom of Harmonious Living for Modern Times, SHAMBALA, BOSTON, 1996.
ISBN 1-57062-100-4

RECOMMENDATIONS

BOOKS

Gallagher, Winifred, The Power of Place-How Our Surroundings Shape Our Thoughts, Emotions, and Actions, FIRST HARPER PERENNIAL, NEW YORK, 1994.
ISBN 0-06-097602-0

Page, Michael, The Power of Chi, EQUARIAN PRESS, SAN FRANCISCO 1988
ISBN 1-85538-363-2

Visconti, Lina, Seven Step Feng Shui, TM PUBLICATIONS, RICHMOND HILL, 1998.
ISBN 0-9684391-0-1

Wong, Eva, Feng-Shui- The Ancient Wisdom of Harmonious Living for Modern Times, SHAMBALA, BOSTON, 1996.
ISBN 1-57062-100-4

MAGAZINES

Feng Shui - Northern Connections
TM PUBLICATIONS , TORONTO, CANADA

Feng Shui for Modern Living
STEPHEN SKINNER, LONDON, ENGLAND

Feng Shui Journal
JAMES ALLYN MOSER, SAN DIEGO, CALFORNIA

WEBSITES

www.fengshuicdn.com
www.astro-fengshui.com
www.qi-whiz.com
www.shambhallafenngshui.com
www.168fengshui.com

ASSOCIATIONS

Feng Shui Association of Canada
FSIC - Registered Practitioners

INSTRUCTION

Feng Shui Institute of Canada
9251-8 Yonge Street, Box 121 Richmond Hill, Greater Toronto Area
Ontario, Canada L4C 9T3
Tel: 416-878-5617 Email: enerchi@yesic.com